Biosocial Synchrony
on Sumba

Biosocial Synchrony on Sumba

Multispecies Relationships and Environmental Variations in Indonesia

Cynthia T. Fowler

LEXINGTON BOOKS
Lanham • Boulder • New York • London

Published by Lexington Books
An imprint of The Rowman & Littlefield Publishing Group, Inc.
4501 Forbes Boulevard, Suite 200, Lanham, Maryland 20706
www.rowman.com

Unit A, Whitacre Mews, 26-34 Stannary Street, London SE11 4AB

Ł   Library Cataloguing in Publication Information Available

The hardback edition of this book was previously catalogued by the Library of Congress as follows:

Library of Congress Cataloging-in-Publication Data

Names: Fowler, Cynthia, 1970- author.
Title: Biosocial synchrony on Sumba : multispecies relationships and environmental
    variations in Indonesia / by Cynthia Fowler.
Description: Lanham : Lexington Books, [2016] | Includes bibliographical references
    and index.
Identifiers: LCCN 2016050376 (print) | LCCN 2016050739 (ebook) |
    ISBN 9781498521840 (cloth : alk. paper) | ISBN 9781498521857 (electronic)
Subjects: LCSH: Kodi (Indonesian people)–Ethnobiology. | Human ecology–
    Indonesia–Kodi. | Sociobiology–Indonesia–Kodi. | Traditional ecological
    knowledge–Indonesia–Kodi. | Ethnology–Indonesia–Kodi.
Classification: LCC DS632.K6 F69 2016 (print) | LCC DS632.K6 (ebook) |
    DDC 304.2089/9922–dc23
LC record available at https://lccn.loc.gov/2016050376

ISBN 9781498521840 (cloth : alk. paper)
ISBN 9781498521864 (pbk. : alk. paper)
ISBN 9781498521857 (electronic)

Printed in the United States of America

For all of the precious animals with whom we share this Earth. Especially, for the plants and animals who are my closest neighbors in the Carolina foothills. For the turkeys, foxes, bears, bobcats, deer, raccoons, possums, frogs, and snakes, may we learn to protect your habitat. For the salamanders, turtles, fishes, and beavers, may we learn to let your water cleanly flow. For the owls, hawks, chimney swifts, barn swallows, bats, kingfishers, egrets, woodpeckers, red cardinals, blue birds, hummingbirds, bees, wasps, grasshoppers, crickets, cicadas, earthworms, and spiders, may we learn how to keep your air free from our pollutants and how to conserve your space.

Contents

Acknowledgments

Deep gratitude to all of my Kodi friends for your willingness to share your knowledge about the animals on your island. My love for you and your home-lands extends to the seaworms, turtles, cuttlefish, sharks, dugong, shellfish, starfish, and the other creatures who inhabit your oceans, reefs, creeks, and reservoirs. My best wishes go out to the macaques, pigs, deer, civets, ˙ e, rats, pythons, pit vipers, geckos, tokays, and skinks. I hope with all ᴏꜰ my heart for the survival of your bats, flying foxes, owls, cockatoos, kestrels, falcons, hawks, buttonquail, song birds, butterflies, and insects.

I regrettably have left out many of animals who inhabit Sumba in these brief acknowledgments. To them I also send my love and well-wishes.

Much love to David J. Cook for his gigantic heart and for being a steadfast source of comic relief and reality checks.

I owe many debts of gratitude to Wofford College for granting a profes-sional leave to write this manuscript. With great humility, I bow my head in thanks for the collegiality of Wofford's faculty and staff with whom I am incredibly grateful to have the opportunity to work.

Many thanks to Kasey Beduhn, Amy King, and the hardworking staff at Lexington Books. I am incredibly grateful to an anonymous reviewer for her gentle critique and generous advice on the first draft of this ethnography.

Cover photo: The peaked rooftops of Sumbanese houses silhouetted by the light from celestial bodies.

Chapter 1

Stretching Our Biosocial Universe

Biosocial Synchrony on Sumba explores our changing world by assessing the space-time dimensions of a biosocial network on the island of Sumba in the Indo-Pacific Warm Pool. Biosocial networks unite distinct human communities, connect humans with diverse nonhuman organisms, link abiotic and biotic entities, bind the living with the previously living, and embed the Earthly in the universal. Change is continuously in motion as the constituents of biosocial networks exchange information, matter, and energy. Biosocial theory holds that some nonhuman species are, like humans, social beings, and that, when humans engage with other living beings and nonliving entities, we all influence each other in biological and social ways. Through the relationships we engage in, all of us together construct biosocieties, which are collectives of interacting entities. Biosocieties and biosocial networks are synonyms, and they are the entanglements of living organisms, nonliving entities, and environmental milieu that are hurling together through space-time.

Our biosocial network spans from the microorganisms within single individuals of specific species out to the cosmic matter in the farthest reaches of our universe. In our ever-expanding universe the relatively tiny biosocieties that we humans inhabit here on Earth are always under construction as "coevolution constantly reshapes interacting species across highly dynamic landscapes" (Thompson 2005: 6). Moreover, as the combination of ethnographic, marine biological, and astronomical evidence in this book demonstrates, the constituents of biosocieties and universes coevolve as they share elements of themselves via their interactions within their complex networks. This book describes space-time relationships in the one particular contemporary community named Kodi that is grounded on the island of Sumba, but whose biosocial networks extend through human bodies and celestial bodies all the way out into the space-time that operates beyond the edges of the universe and back again to Kodi.

While "Kodi" is an analytical and narrative device as well as an Indigenous ethnolinguistic category, Kodi is also an actual biosocial network. As a biosocial network, Kodi is a collection of interacting entities. The entities engage in social relationships with one another in ways that define them biologically as organisms and ecologically as communities. The interconnections between biotic and abiotic entities define the compositions, structures, and functions of individuals, categories, human communities, and ecological networks (Olff et al. 2009). Some relationships between some entities cause those entities to materially substantiate one another. *Biosocial Synchrony on Sumba* demonstrates the content of the biosocieties composed of individuals, categories, and communities who coevolve by focusing on the especially substantive relationships between humans and polychaetes (chapters 2 and 3), and humans and celestial bodies (chapters 4 and 5).

Biosocial Synchrony on Sumba is inspired by the extraordinarily fascinating social and natural world of Kodi, and also by recent developments in anthropological theory and in the environmental sciences. Ideas taken from Kodi perceptions of the world align remarkably well with anthropologists' interpretations of social change and environmental scientists' findings on ecological dynamics. Throughout this book, readers will find ethnography, theory, and ecology woven together as I attempt to relay information about socioecological change. Indigenous Kodi people's knowledge about the biota and abiota of their homelands is not substitutable with another other social group's knowledge. We can learn more about ecological relationships in Kodi from the people who trace their lineages many generations back to communities who have lived in Kodi than we can from any other source. But, we can best establish the context for that local knowledge and those local relationships by relying on what social theorists and environmental scientists reveal about the dynamic, complex, emerging contexts within which biota and abiota live and also about the biological, behavioral, and social lives of the biota and abiota themselves.

DOCUMENTING LOCAL KNOWLEDGE AND BORROWING FROM SCIENTIFIC DISCIPLINES

Researchers who want to investigate the biosocial relationships between humans, nonhuman organisms, and environments need to know not only about humans but also about other organisms and environments, and thus need to integrate information from multiple disciplines. *Biosocial Synchrony on Sumba* illustrates the necessity of interdisciplinary work when studying biosocial becomings. In my attempts to apply biosocial theory to the study of socioecological change on Sumba, I use ethnography to gather anthropological data, draw information from marine biology to explain human-polychaete interactions, and borrow from astronomy to demonstrate the depth and breadth of biosocial networks. While *Biosocial Synchrony on Sumba* draws on the methodologies of several disciplines, at its heart is the ethnographic fieldwork that I have done myself with the goal of documenting how people and the other living beings in a semiarid, monsoonal, tropical biome become (i.e., change over space-time) through "action-in-relationality" (Pitrou 2015, under "An Anthropology Beyond Nature and Culture?"). My field work in 1997–1998, 2007, 2008, and 2014 involved collecting data about human-environment interactions using participant observation, ethnobiological inventories, environmental sampling, and spatial mapping.

I have done in Kodi what other scholars have done in their attempts to understand biosocial becomings: "map the configurations within which human and non-human agents interact, constitute themselves, establish mutual relations, are formed, etc." (Pitrou 2015, under "An Anthropology Beyond Nature and Culture?"). I have observed how Kodi agropastoralists and fishers physically interact with their abiotic companions by watching, listening, and assisting them with their work tending crops, raising livestock, harvesting and hunting wild land and ocean species, and accessing potable water. I have participated in their daily activities by accompanying them as they traverse their landscapes, working with them in their gardens, going with them to bathing holes and toting water back home, visiting relatives with them, buying and selling items in marketplaces, firing gardens and grasslands, and collecting resources from the full range of the region's ecosystems. In innumerable interviews, Kodi agropastoralists and fishers have shared with me their place-based ecological knowledge, their representations of themselves and their relationships with the living and nonliving world, their perceptions of their worlds, their political viewpoints, and their desires for themselves and their loved ones. Through deep hanging out (Geertz 1998) in Kodi and intensive data analysis, I have developed ideas about how Kodi identities and biophysicalities are mutually constituted. Because I have been studying the Kodi biosociety for nearly twenty years, I have had the opportunity to witness some changes in people and places and also to learn about the changes that Kodi residents have witnessed themselves. These methodologies have enabled me to write this book about biosocial change in the Kodi region on the Indonesian island of Sumba and the deeper biosocial field which we all occupy together.

My hope for this book is that it expands the purview of biosocial theory beyond the human to the realms outside of the Earth's atmosphere and beyond. I forsee this book as provoking a postoikos dialogue by joining in scholarly conversations about human perceptions of, experiences within, cognition of, and knowledge about the world, and contributing to stimulating conversations about the "anthropology of life" (Ingold 2013; Keck 2013; Kohn 2013; Pitrou 2015). The monograph begins participating in the provocations in chapters 2 and 3 with an exploration of the construction of human knowledge about biosocial worlds via an illustration of the ways biosocial relationships in multispecies communities compose and change space-time with special attention to the colorful interactions between people and polychaetes (also known as marine worms or seaworms). Next in chapters 4 and 5, this book showcases a select few enlightening links between Earthly and celestial bodies, and thereby exposes the embeddedness of Earthbound multispecies communities within a roving biosocial universe with immense space-time dimensions.

A VERY DEEP FIELD

Our vast universe is the context for this study of the space-time dimensions of biosocial change where a multiplicity of biotic and abiotic agents are incessantly moving together, pushing and pulling on each other's matter, and exchanging matter, information, and energy with one another. Space and time are inseparable in reality, though they are frequently parsed for analytical purposes. All of the universe's constituents embody, index, and express their experiences with motion, matter, and energy, though we manifest our experiences in diverse ways. Space-time is in motion relative to the observer, and our perception of it varies depending on the observer's characteristics. Humans have more or less capacity to sensorily and cognitively access the ways nonhumans and nonliving agents manifest their environmental experiences. This is the case because of our biological inheritances and also our social statuses. The space-time culture within which we are exposed to the motion, matter, information, and energy of our coexistents influences how we sense and know. For example, as this book shows, our space-time cultures affect whether we chant, play drums, and inspect chicken entrails as the means for "talking" with the Moon and Sun as the Kodi people do, or whether we use beam splitters, mirrors, and vibration isolation systems, to hear gravitational waves or cameras, telescopes, and satellites to see astronomical objects as U.S.-based astrophysicists do.

This book demonstrates that all of the universe's coexistents embody, index, and express this universe by profiling a select few of the universe's special nonhuman agents: namely, polychaetes, the Moon, and the Sun. These starring characters are companions to a panoply of agential living and nonliving, human and nonhuman, Earthbound and extraterrestrial entities who populate a literal deep field that extends from the Earth's surface out into the far reaches of the sky and back again. "Deep field" is a loan concept from the term "Hubble Deep Field" (HDF) which is a montage of images captured by the Wide Field and Planetary Camera aboard the Hubble Space Telescope in 1995. In our "deepest-ever" (Williams 1996, under "About this Image") view, we can see all the way to the horizon of the universe. HDF makes visible for the first time in human history millions of celestial bodies, including galaxies whose "shapes and colors . . . are important clues to understanding the evolution of the universe" (Williams 1996, under "About this Image").

The stage where this book's main characters act is a figurative "deep field" too because my analysis of this metaphorical theater contributes, I hope, to the vibrant theoretical push for "a paradigm shift of a consequence for the human sciences of the twenty-first century equal to or greater than that which the Darwinian paradigm had for the sciences of the twentieth" (Ingold 2013: 2). Myself and other participants who are "beginning to converge on a synthesis—at once processual, developmental and relational" (Ingold 2013: 20) are forcing a "fundamental revision of what we mean by humanity, evolution, culture and social life" (Ingold 2013: 20). Recent disruptions appear under numerous banners: biosocial (Ingold 2013), anthropology of life (Ingold 2013; Kohn 2013), transspecies (Kohn 2007), multispecies (Kirksey, Schuetze, and Helmreich 2014), posthumanism (Whitehead 2009), and cannibal metaphysics (Viveiros de Castro 2014). The historical precedents for these newish titles are in ethnobiology, environmental anthropology, poststructuralism, transcendental empiricism, and other convergent endeavors. My thinking brings together these older and newer teachings in a biosocial-phenomenological-cognitive methodology. This integrative framework helps me explain how all of us coexistents collectively construct biosocial worlds. Within this framework, "construct" means the cultural-discursive-historical-geographical invention of cosmologies as well as and as equally important as the manufacturing of biological-geophysical-embodied realities. As this book shows, cultural cosmologies and biophysical realities are mutually constituted.

Bringing the biosocial-phenomenological-cognitive framework to astronomy means casting that discipline's objects as humans' in-flight companions. It means considering equivalencies: such possibilities as celestial bodies' capacities to communicate and humans' capacity to hear what they say, and see what they are. Astronomical objects and phenomena communicate in gravitational waves and cosmic radiation. Humans can easily sense some of the communications, such as visible light, tidal fluctuations, and daily, seasonal, and annual rhythms. For other astronomical objects, though, we cannot easily sense them, but some of us (i.e., astrophysicists and consumers of their publications) can detect their messages. An example is the dark matter making up 90 percent of the universe's matter whose "bodies" are invisible to our eyes but who we know have "pronounced effects on the formation and evolution of galaxies and clusters of galaxies" (Tyson, Liu, and Irion 2000, under "Dark Matter"). Integrating biosocial with astronomical theory involves using "clues" from extraterrestrial worlds and information about the evolution of the universe as evidence for explaining Earth's space-time cultures and the co-becoming of humans with all of the universe's nonhuman constituents.

The project of *Biosocial Synchrony on Sumba* to understand the processes of change in biosocieties, follows efforts within social theory to deconstruct the kinds of understandings of evolution that deemphasize emergent and developmental processes. The dynamic understanding of evolution that forms the premise of this book is taken from Ingold's theory of biosocial becomings. Ingold defines evolution as follows: "[Evolution] can only be understood topologically, as the unfolding of the entire tapestry—of the all-embracing matrix of relationships wherein the manifold forms of life that we call 'cultural' emerge and are held in place. Within this matrix, the becoming of every constituent both conditions and is conditioned by the becoming of other constituents to which it relates" (Ingold 2013: 8).

Biosocial theory provides a framework for investigating change in biosocial networks that relies on an updated version of evolutionary theory and the more full-bodied understanding of the relationships between humans, nonhuman organisms, and environmental milieu. Evolution is a classic topic and one of the fundamental theories of the human and environmental sciences. Biosocial theory allows researchers to continue using evolutionary theory, but in ways that are enhanced by current understandings of development, plasticity, emergence, niche construction, ecological inheritance, and coevolution. Organisms are generated through their genetic inheritances as well as their ecological inheritances and their sociocultural upbringing. Organisms are born into environmental milieu with particular genetic traits and are shaped throughout their life-long development through the interactions between their genetic traits, phenotypes, ecological affordances and limitations, and their social circumstances. Landscapes and their abiotic components are involved in coevolution too—in addition to living organisms—since organisms and populations modify their habitats in the course of their lives and over multiple generations. The qualities of organisms' biophysical environments and the traits of their biotic companions (including other humans) in those environments influence the organisms' own development. Recognizing plasticity in the development of organisms enables researchers to focus on the relationships, to analyze habitats in terms of relational ecologies, and to think in terms of the mutual substantiation of organisms and landscapes. Organisms who influence one another's development are engaged in mutual substantiation, which, over time, leads to the coevolution of populations.

In coevolution, "reciprocal evolutionary change shapes interspecific interactions" (Thompson 2005: 3).

MAMMALIA-POLYCHAETA-LUNA-SOL

Biosocial Synchrony on Sumba illustrates how the incorporation of phenomenological and cognitive concerns can enhance biosocial theory in recognition of the capacity among many organisms to sense their environments, communicate about their experiences, and construct their cognitive and biophysical worlds. The main characters in this book—humans, polychaetes, the Moon, and the Sun—are ecosystem engineers who play significant roles in constructing their biophysical and social worlds. The actions and activities of numerous organisms cause physical changes in habitats, and these organisms are thus ecosystem engineers (Jones, Lawton, and Shachak 1994; Wright and Jones 2006) Notable examples of ecosystem engineers are nitrogen-fixing plants (Vitousek et al. 1987), beavers, elephants, pigs (Singer et al. 1984), aquatic algae (Zulkifly et al. 2013), reef-forming mollusks, benthic seagrass (Meadows, Meadows, and Murray 2012), intertidal kelp (Burnaford, Nielsen, and Williams 2014), marine benthic worms (Wright and Jones 2006), and earthworms. Polychaetes, the main characters of chapters 2 and 3, are ecosystem engineers in the ocean benthos (Wright and Jones 2006), similar to the ways earthworms engineer soils (Darwin 1881) in terrestrial environments. Polychaetes also engineer human ritual practices together with multiple other species and nonliving entities. The Moon and Sun are ecosystem engineers (Burnaford, Neilsen, and Williams 2014) of the Earth and vice versa. Lunar cycles affect Earth's ocean tides and sea levels (Burnaford, Nielsen, and Williams 2014); modify the reproductive biology of plants, invertebrates and other species living in tidal zones, including polychaetes; interact with human reproductive biology; and influence the ways humans organize time and their ritual calendars.

Just as some types of organisms are more powerful ecological engineers than others, some types of organisms are more social than others. Microbes, ants, bees, and dogs are some of the nonhuman creatures who are characterized as being social creatures. People and polychaetes too are social both with members of their own species and with other species. When they form discernible assemblages, people and polychaetes and the other species with whom they are entangled form biosocieties. This book shows how a select subnetwork of ecosystem engineers—people, polychaetes, the Moon, and the Sun—shapes Kodi's seascapes and landscapes and influences change in seascapes and landscapes.

The initial reason polychaetes, the Moon, and the Sun became important characters in *Biosocial Synchrony on Sumba* is because their relationships with humans are incredibly fascinating and their role in Kodi space-time culture is absolutely compelling. While humans communicate mainly through human language and paralanguage, nonhumans communicate in various non-discursive and/or discursive modalities. Nonhumans signify via light, color, shape, movement, activity, sounds and vocalizations. Some species of polychaetes and some other marine species bioluminesce to communicate about matters related to reproduction, predation, and survival. Bioluminescent organisms embody and express their relationships with their coexistents and their experiences in their environments with astounding brilliance.

In the fully lived context of Kodi biosociety, though, polychaetes are merely one among numerous possible animals that could serve to prove the centrality of human-animal relationships in constructing Kodi's biosocial niches. Water buffalo, horses, pigs, and chickens are extraordinarily valuable symbolically and economically in the lives of Kodi agropastoralists, as are diverse other nonhuman wild and domesticated animals. But, here in this book, the spotlight falls on the polychaetes. In a biosocial frame the value of polychaetes is inestimable. Polychaete specialists, marine biologists, and anthropologists attest to the merit of polychaetes. Polychaete specialists have found information in their research about the life history, habitat, and reproductive behaviors of polychaetes that helps explain human-polychaete interactions in Kodi and in many other communities across the Indo-Pacific. An example that provides a brief foreshadowing to the content in chapters 2 and 3 is that polychaetes breed and human communities perform ritual gatherings of polychaetes in synchrony with lunar periodicity.

In drawing attention to the multispecies interactions that sometimes occur when polychaetes swarm in ritual sites, this biosocial study could inspire marine biologists to recognize the ways anthropology can contribute to marine biology. At the local level, marine biologists could consult ethnographies to determine the specific date ranges and specific reefs where polychaetes breed because islanders' rituals coincide with seaworm swarmings. This could help polychaete specialists better target when and where they could observe, identify, conduct species inventories, and otherwise study polychaetes. Chapter 3 of this ethnography contains a brief comparative analysis of spatial variations throughout the Indo-Pacific in ethnotaxonomies for "seaworms," communities who perform seaworm rituals, and seaworm swarming times, which could help guide polychaete specialists on when and where to conduct their research. Ethnographic information could guide polychaete specialists to polychaete swarms where they could measure the multiple factors that cause and affect seaworm swarming by examining water temperatures, tide levels, currents, water composition and quality, wind, light, and other conditions that might inform them about the range of reproductive behaviors in polychaetes.

While polychaete biologists record the incredible diversity and fascinating behaviors of a very special class of marine fauna, ethnography provides a framework for producing a rich understanding of biosocial processes. Historical linguistics and colonial documents attest to the deep history of human-polychaete bonds. For a very long time Sumbanese Islanders have been constructing their biosocial worlds while interacting with polychaetes and the many other species in their communities. Polychaetes may have been interacting with Austronesian peoples on Sumba's reefs for as long as 4,800 years and they may have been interacting with Papuan peoples on Sumba's reefs for much longer, possibly 14,000 years (Lansing et al. 2007). Ocean reefs are intriguing sites for exploring relationships between marine organisms, humans, and the abiotic environment. Research in coevolutionary theory suggests that coral reefs "rely upon coevolved symbioses between corals and zooanthellae and upon additional interactions between corals and algae-feeding fish, although how coevolution has shaped some of these interactions is still poorly understood" (Thompson 2005: 5). This book's descriptions of the interactions between reef substrates, marine organisms, people, and celestial bodies provides ideas for furthering coevolutionary theory.

For many generations, human-polychaete interactions have been crucial forces in the construction of seascapes, landscapes, and cultures on Sumba. Unfortunately, human-seaworm-multispecies communities on Sumba nowadays face many threats. Overexploitation from commercial fishing threatens to reduce marine biodiversity. Global warming threatens to change marine habitats. A recent wave of land grabbing on Sumba threatens to remove spawning sites as well as other beaches and reefs from traditional tenure and resource management regimes, and threatens to degrade people's sacred places and polychaetes' breeding sites. If seaworm populations were to decline or breeding practices were to change because of anthropogenic and climatic processes, polychaete breeding patterns could alter, long-standing local practices could shift, and the human-seaworm bond could deteriorate.

Ethnographic evidence shows that seaworms continue to be crucial for the wellbeing of contemporary communities in the Indo-Pacific region. The human-polychaete bond has endured for so long on Sumba because people continue to believe in and practice the Indigenous Marapu religion, because Marapu followers have had continuous access to and have continuously collected resources from seaworm swarming sites, and because seaworms continue to breed on the island's tidal reefs. All three of these conditions are tentative. None of them is guaranteed for the future.

The integration of anthropological data about human-polychaete interactions with information about polychaetes from marine biology, and about changing marine ecosystems from other disciplines could be applied to constructing equitable management programs for polychaete swarming sites that could maximize the potential for sustaining polychaete populations at levels where they could continue contributing to the biophysical, emotional, and cultural wellbeing of Kodi people in the face of accelerated environmental change. The knowledge that Kodi people have about polychaetes is both inherently valuable and also could potentially be used in the conservation of corals, polychaetes, other reef species, the reefs themselves, and other ocean ecosystems nearshore and farther from shores. Anthropological information about local ecological knowledge combined with scientific data about polychaetes could be used to support the establishment of marine conservation areas at seaworm swarming sites.

A LENGTHY AND MOVING TRANSECT

Biosocial Synchrony on Sumba is about how Kodi construct their cosmological and ecological worlds in collaboration with the diverse biota and abiota who co-inhabit their biosocial network. For humans, constructing worlds involves sensing, perceiving, and cognizing which create experiences and knowledges. Sensing, perceiving, and cognizing occur when we are co-mobile with the vast variety of other entities who co-inhabit our biosocial universe. Our experiences within and knowledges of the world are always constructed when we are in motion. We are always moving even though our sensors may signal to us that we are sitting still or in some steady state.

The whole universe is continuously moving, and we are moving together with it. Our Earth is continuously rotating at 1,000 miles per hour on its axis, while at the same time the Earth is revolving around the Sun at 66,000 miles per hour, while the Sun (and thus Earth) circles around the Milky Way Galaxy at 483,000 miles per hour, at the same time as the solar system spirals at 43,000 miles per hour through the Milky Way toward the star Vega (Franknoi 2007), and the Milky Way rushes toward Leo and Virgo at 1.3 million miles per hour. This entire network is connected to an unknown number of moving galaxies in a moving universe.

While our capacities to sense the world around us are somewhat limited, by manipulating our perspectives we can broaden our experiences and knowledges of the universe. This book shifts our perspectives numerous times as it describes a biosocial network from the perspectives of marine worms to the viewpoints of worm worshippers in chapters 2 and 3, and from celestial bodies to human bodies in chapters 4 and 5. Manipulating our perspectives is a simple technique for learning more about immensely complex biosocial processes. The technique yields basic information about Sumba's seascapes and landscapes and human-nonhuman interactions. And the technique helps us to answer basic questions about biosocial change, multispecies interactions, and synchrony. By shifting perspectives, we learn more about "cycles of contingency" (Laland 2013: 433) and the "interacting cascades" (Laland 2013: 433) whereby humans and their biotic and abiotic companions coevolve.

Biosocial Synchrony on Sumba unites scientific and local knowledges (Crumley 2007) to better grasp how "reciprocal causation" (Laland 2013: 433) between humans and environments have constructed the ecological inheritances (Odling-Smee, Laland, and Feldman 2013) we can witness now in Kodi. Although linking local to global processes is an extremely difficult task (Crumley 2007) because the complexity of biosocial networks is "daunting" (Van Wey, Ostrom, and Meretsky 2005: 49), *Biosocial Synchrony on Sumba* links patterns and processes across multiple spatial and temporal levels using a framework that contains a broad spectrum of theories and methods ranging from the entrenched and innovative Earth sciences to critical and engaged biosocial theory.

Across the academic disciplines, research efforts to understand anthropogenic contributions to global change are plentiful. This study originated in anthropology and extends into marine biology and astronomy. Ethnography tells us about humans, marine biology tells us about polychaetes, and astronomy teaches us about the Earth-Moon system within the context of the solar system and the universe. Combining these sciences into a story about biosocial relationships in Kodi has produced a study of multispecies interactions along a transect that begins on the floor of the ocean where seaworms dwell and stretches to the horizon of the universe.

The inclination to never stop changing and to keep on moving pervades the entire biosocial network and its momentum carries along all of its constituents whether or not they do so with conscious intent. Kodi's biosocial network has been evolving and will continue to emerge through continuous feedback between ecological and social processes. Change in contemporary biosocieties flows forth from the interactions between biotic and abiotic components of ecosystems. Biosocieties and their components embody their ecological inheritances. This state of things poses many opportunities to explore questions about what Kodi's biosocial worlds look like, why they look that way, and what the human influence has been. Approaching questions about what changes are happening and why from varying perspectives yields more holistic understandings of space-time, and leads to the discovery of the spectacular multispecies interactions that are part of the change processes in biosocial networks, such as synchrony.

SYNCHRONY IN INTRASPECIES AND INTERSPECIES INTERACTIONS

The title of this book highlights the concept of synchrony because it is a fundamental type of multispecies interaction that occurs in Kodi's biosocial network. Synchrony shapes the composition and function of those ecological communities where it occurs and influences the dynamics of environmental processes. Synchrony exists in some of the interactions that occur between some biotics and abiotics, between populations of distinct species, and between subpopulations of species (Koenig et al. 1999). The example of synchrony that is the subject of this book involves correlations between abiotic factors and biotic factors, and between biota who belong to the distinct Classes of Mammalia and Polychaeta. Thus this book illustrates an example of inter-taxa synchrony where the taxa are distinct Classes (Mammalia and Polychaeta) and discrete factors (biotic and abiotic).

Synchrony is covariation in the biologies and behaviors of organisms. Synchrony occurs in the population demographics, reproductive behaviors, feeding patterns, and niche construction activities of numerous species interactions. Depending on the species and contextual forces, a population's subunits may exhibit demographic correlations in reproduction, birthrates, mortality, mean size, mean age, sex ratios, migration and dispersal, and population densities. Reproductive synchrony may occur among individuals of the same species, between subpopulations of a single species, and also between populations of different species (Koenig et al. 1999; Leibhold, Koenig, and Bjørnstad 2004). Reproductive synchrony within species is the "tendency of s̃ me individuals to carry out some stage of their reproductive cycle at the s̃ time as other members of the population" (Weiser 1999: 112). Since 195̃ when Moran linked the population dynamics of Canadian lynx to environmental variations, researchers have documented synchrony in manifold taxa. A multitude of mammals, plants, fish, mollusks, amphibians, birds, insects, fungi, and viruses are involved in synchronies with members of their own species or other species.

Stability and instability in ecological communities is associated with asynchrony and synchrony in consumer-resource and predator-prey relationships. Asynchronic interactions means that covariations do not occur in species biologies, behaviors, and population patterns, while synchronic interactions means that covariations do occur. Asynchronous population densities among consumers that compete for the same resources and predators' preferences for prey among the competing consumers leads to community stability in some constant environments. Synchronous behaviors and population densities among competing consumers can lead to the depletion of the common food resources of competing consumers, declines in population densities, migration, or other adjustments (Loreau and Mazancourt 2008). Multispecies interactions can shift between synchronic and asynchronic over time due to internal and external forces. Examples of shifts in multispecies interactions and environmental contexts that affect synchrony are: plant phenology relative to the temporality of cold exposure; plant phenology relative to insect pollination and herbivore predation; timing of snow-melt; and photoperiod (Wilmer 2012).

Environmental variations partially explain synchrony in biosocial networks. For example, lynx populations positively respond to snowfall increases, while lynx populations negatively respond to rainfall increases. The Southern Oscillation Index decreases rainfall, thereby positively impacting lynx populations while negatively impacting their prey snowshoe hare populations. Northern hemispheric temperatures and the North Atlantic Oscillation increase rainfall, reduce snowfall, thereby negatively impacting lynx populations and positively impacting snowshoe hare populations (Yan et al. 2013). Another example is the synchronic fluctuations in the fruiting of pistachio trees, which correlates with variations in weather conditions (Rosenstock et al. 2011).

Numerous types of environmental variations, fluctuations, or changes act as mechanisms to induce synchrony and/or lead to shifts between synchrony and asynchrony. In response to external factors, synchronic interactions sometimes remain synchronic and sometimes shift to asynchronic interactions. The biologies of distinct species that are coupled in synchronic behaviors may become uncoupled due to environmental change, which may delink some of the key threads that bind biosocieties into networks. A/synchrony and the mechanisms that induce a/synchrony operate at local, regional, and global scales. Among the numerous known mechanisms that influence synchrony are:

- climate and weather fluctuations
  - warming and drying trends
  - precipitation fluctuations (Koenig et al. 1999)
  - air temperature variations (Koenig et al. 1999)
  - sea surface temperature variations (Cheal et al. 2007)
- climate oscillations
  - El Niño-Southern Oscillation (Cheal et al. 2007)
  - North Atlantic Oscillation (Yan et al. 2013)
- seasonality
  - seasonal forcing (Earn, Rohani, and Grenfell 1998)
- lunar periodicity
- solar periodicity
- wind speed (Cheal et al. 2007)
- tides
- ocean currents
- habitat fragmentation (Wilmer 2012)
- movement ecologies
  - dispersal (Moran 1953)

  ○ subpopulation migrations
  ○ exotic species migrations
* trophic interactions
* shifting plant and animal phenologies

Globally, interspecies and intraspecies synchrony exists in both land and ocean ecosystems, in wild and domesticated populations. Synchrony operates in a variety of environments ranging from coral reef ecosystems (Cheal et al. 2007) to agroecosystems (Rosenstock et al. 2011), and from boreal forests (Yan et al. 2007) to oak stands in Mediterranean climates (Koenig et al. 1999). To this list we might add that synchrony operates in the tidal zones and semiarid landscapes that compose Sumba's island communities.

Numerous species of marine organisms living in tropical reefs synchronize reproductive behaviors, feeding activities, and space-time movements with tidal patterns and lunar cycles (Cheal et al. 2007; Weiser 1999). The reef-inhabiting organisms' abilities to sense changes in the water and light (Weiser 1999) influence their behavioral responses to environmental cues. Synchrony is associated with numerous environmental variations in coral reef ecosystems, including the tides, currents, sea surface temperature, and wind (Cheal et al. 2007).

Spatial synchrony is the autocorrelation of space-time where the autocorrelation of variation occurs spatially (like it does in the general category of synchrony) and also temporally (Leibhold, Koenig, and Bjørnstad 2004). Some biota and abiota that are in proximity to one another may exhibit spatial synchrony (Leibhold, Koenig, and Bjørnstad 2004), and subpopulations of numerous spatially-dispersed species exhibit spatial synchrony. The "values" of abiotic processes such as elevation, air temperature, and sea surface temperature "at nearby locations tend to be similar" (Leibhold, Koenig, and Bjørnstad 2004: 468), and thus exert a relatively uniform force upon the organisms or populations who live nearby one another. Spatial synchrony may exist in the Kodi biosocial network where people, polychaetes, and their companions respond to similar external forces.

Synchrony is intraspecies when individuals of the same species correlate, interspecies when populations of different species correlate, or both. Some of the taxa who engage in intraspecies synchrony are:

* Canada lynx (*Lynx canadensis*) (Moran 1953)
* coral reef inhabitants
  ○ corals (Harrison et al. 1984)
  ○ damselfish (*Pomacentrus*) (Cheal et al. 2007)
  ○ labrid fishes (e.g., *Thallasoma* sp.) (Victor et al. 2001)
* polychaetes (Polychaeta) (e.g., Caspers 1984)
* olive ridley turtles (*Lepidochelys olivacea*) (Plotkin et al. 1997)

- sea cucumbers (*Patinapta ooplax*) (Kubota 2005)
- sea urchins (*Centrostephanus coronatus*) (Kennedy and Pearse 1975)
- crabs (Ocypodidae and Grapsidae) (Scov et al. 2005)
- California tiger salamanders (*Ambystoma californiense*)
- field voles (*Microtus arvalis*) (Mackin-Rogalska and Nabaglo 1990)
- beech caterpillars (*Quadricalcalifera punctatella*) (Leibhold, Kamata, and Jacob 1996)
- western tent caterpillars (*Malacisoma californicum pluviale*) (Myers 1990)
- cicadas (Cicadidae) (Williams, Smith, and Stephen 1994)
- katydids (*Neoconocephalus ensiger*) (Murphy, Thompson, and Shul 2016)
- fireflies (e.g., *Photinus carolinus*, *Photuris* spp.) (Copeland and Moiseff 1994; Lewis, Faust, and De Cock 2012)
- grouse (*Tetrao* spp. and *Bonasa* sp.) (Lindström, Ranta, and Linden 1996)
- goshawk nestlings (*Accipiter gentiles*)
- oaks (Koenig et al. 1999)
- pistachios (Rosenstock et al. 2011)

Examples of taxa who perform interspecies synchrony are:

- predators and prey
  - Canada lynx (*Lynx canadensis*) and snowshoe hares (*Lepus americanus*) in Canada's boreal forest (Yan et al. 2013)
- resources and consumers
  - mast-producing oaks, the mammals who consume the mast, and the gypsy moths (*Lymantria dyspar*) whose primary predators are the mast-eating mammals
  - beech trees and the herbivorous *Epirrita autumnata* moth
- plants and their pollinators (Wilmer 2012)
- parasites and their hosts
- oaks (Koenig et al. 1999)
- polychaetes

Some taxa are simultaneously involved in both intraspecies and interspecies synchrony. A botanical example comes from California's coastal region where several species of oaks synchronize mast seeding with oaks in their same species as well as with oaks belonging to other species (Koenig et al. 1999). An example from the ocean world is the intraspecies and interspecies synchrony in the reproductive biology of polychaetes. Individual polychaetes swarm to spawn at the same time and in the same locations as other individuals within their species, and numerous species can be found in some spawning swarms (Pamungkas and Glasby 2015).

Based on what we do know about polychaete reproduction in general (for details see chapters 2 and 3) together with what we know about synchrony in other coral reef species, we could reasonably hypothesize that intraspecies synchrony exists in at least some of Sumba's polychaete populations. Regarding interspecies synchrony, it might exist between distinct species of polychaetes in the waters around Sumba, and even possibly with nonpolychaetes. We have no information about interspecies synchrony in the population dynamics of polychaetes and people on Sumba. Instead, we might safely assume that Mammalia and Polychaeta population dynamics are independent of one another (Loureau and Mazancourt 2008). Yet, a different type of synchrony—different than in their population ecologies—might be operating between polychaetes, people, and celestial bodies, and their other companions in Kodi's biosocial network. What kind of synchrony exists between Mammalia and Polychaeta, and between biotics and abiotics in Kodi?

The synchrony in Kodi is a biosocial type, meaning that biological and social correlations function in the people-polychaete-Moon-Sun network, and that environmental and cultural mechanisms induce synchrony. The environmental mechanisms include climate and weather variations, plant, animal, and fungi phenologies, trophic interactions, astronomical cycles, and movements. The cultural mechanisms include sensing and observing synchronies, constructing knowledge about synchronies, symbolizing synchronies, organizing space-time culture around synchronies, and participating in other species' synchronies. The latter points toward the social dimension of Sumba's people-polychaete correlations. Sumbanese people desire to socialize with coral reef species, and they find the times when polychaetes swarm on Sumba's reefs to be the right occasions to participate in seaworms' social lives. Socialization involves physical interactions in a predator-prey or resource-consumer relationship, and it also involves abstract interactions in symbolizer-symbol or worshiper-icon relationships. (Chapters 2 through 5 elaborate on these interactions and relationships.) The trophic interactions, spiritual connections, and other engagements are formational in biosocial networks.

Though numerous synchronic and asynchronic interactions likely occur in Kodi, the long-term, biosocial, sequential synchronic interaction between people, polychaetes, and the Moon and Sun is the subject of this book. This book does not comment on synchrony in polychaete populations since I have collected no data on the subject. What I do have is ethnographic data about interactions between polychaetes and people, which includes ethnobiological data about local knowledge of polychaetes. The data that I have do not support an argument for the classical synchrony where "[d]emographic properties of populations (e.g., abundance and reproduction) often fluctuate synchronously across space and time" (Rosenstock et al. 2011: 1434). We have little evidence for or against correlations in the populations of people and polychaetes on Sumba or anywhere else in the world.

The ethnographic and ethnobiological data reveal the presence of a form of intertaxa synchrony between people, polychaetes, the Moon, and the Sun; a type of synchrony that operates in addition to, the classical one seen in population ecology. The synchronic relationship between these entities actually involves many other associated organisms, abiotics, and processes; including the ocean, reefs, tides, and the diverse marine organisms that swarm together with the seaworms and that people bring with them to seaworm rituals.

A few of the key environmental variations that are associated with synchrony in multispecies interactions generally (i.e., not specifically in Kodi or specifically in people-polychaete-Moon-Sun relationships) and that are part of the equation in Kodi's biosocial network are: (1) lunar periodicity with its accompanying tidal and spectral fluctuations; (2) the wet northeasterly and dry southwesterly Asia-Australia Monsoon with its variable winds and precipitation levels; (3) strong seasonal fluctuations between the wet (November–March) and dry (May–September) segments of the year; and (4) the Indo-Pacific Warm Pool.

Synchrony in Kodi's multispecies communities manifests in the movement ecologies—and not necessarily the population ecologies—of people, polychaetes, celestial bodies, and other entities. When the Earth-Moon-Sun system positions its members in just the right way, the light (and other factors as discussed in upcoming chapters) triggers the seaworms to move into breeding swarms. When the seaworms move to the sea surface above coral reefs and cluster into breeding swarms, Kodi ritual seaworm coll.n-ers swarm the reefs to collect the resource. In general, "the abundance and movement of mobile predator or prey species can synchronize the other" (Rosenstock et al. 2011: 1434). Perhaps this applies to Kodi where the seaworms are the prey and people are their predators in a ritualized trophic web. Rosenstock et al. (2011: 1434) write, "the most compelling examples of these effects [of predator-prey abundance and movement] come from deciduous forests where population fluctuations of seed production, insects, and their predators are well timed." The space-time correlation between people, polychaetes, and the Moon and Sun in coral reefs is equally compelling (Bentley, Olive, and Last 1999). Kodi people synchronize their romantic activities with seaworm spawning by designating the seaworm season as a special time to court lovers in night time rendezvous on the beaches. When Kodi priests engage in intimate relations with the Seaworm Goddess, they use ritual to coordinate a type of spiritual reproduction with the seaworms' biological reproduction.

The spatiotemporal correlation that occurs between the swarming of seaworms, lunar cycles, ambient light, the ritual gatherings of Kodi agropastoralists, crop ripening, seasonality, etc. is an example of biosocial synchrony. To point out the spatiotemporal correlations between these nodes in Kodi's biosocial network is not to suggest that everything people and polychaetes do is synchronous or that synchrony organizes the entire network. Instead, evoking synchrony suggests that in specific places at specific times the interactions between the specific agents who are the subjects of this book "may be sufficient to result in synchrony" (Leibhold, Koenig, and Bjørnstad 2004: 478).

In the island community of Kodi, synchrony is one of the mechanisms that binds living organisms, nonliving entities, and environmental processes into a biosocial network that is constantly changing. In some environments that have experienced mild disturbances, synchrony in multispecies relationships is associated with community stability (Loreau and Mazancourt 2008). In other ecosystems, synchrony in multispecies relationships is an outcome of anthropogenic or non-anthropogenic environmental change. Kodi's biosocial network is both: its disturbance ecology defines its socioecological landscapes (Fowler 2013), yet it also exhibits some persistence in its social and ecological systems, as is evident in the long-term relationships that exist between people, polychaetes, and the Moon and Sun.

The concept of synchrony enables us to explain multispecies interactions and biosocial change in Sumba Island's communities. Synchrony provides insights into the multispecies interactions that occur between people and polychaetes on Sumba as well as in the numerous comparable island communities in Eastern Indonesia, Melanesia, and Polynesia where space-time cultures involve polychaetes. Synchrony explains correlations between human and nonhuman organisms' behaviors and how they align with environmental variations.

Chapter 2

Making Worlds with Transtaxa
Beings in Multispecies Swarms

SEAWORM LAND BITTER LAND

Kodi affectionately refer to their territory as *tana nale* (land of the seaworms). *Tana nale* is sometimes paired with the term *tana pad'du* (bitter land [my translation]) or land of the planting rites (Hoskins's [1998] translation). One way to think about *tana nale tana pad'du* is in the way similar ritual couplets are spoken by people living in Eastern Indonesia: as "paired metaphor[s]r of complementarity and difference" (McWilliam 2006: 267). Another way to think about it is as a categorical continuum; that is, a category of entities who occupy a continuum of types along which they move. *Tana nale tana pad'du* is the entity that moves through space and time as it maneuvers along the continuum from being bitter, irritating, and taboo to being bland, edible, and proscribed. *Tana nale tana pad'du* is land, a biogeophysical entity, and it is also territory attached to a sociocultural identity. *Tana nale* is similar to but different from *tana pad'du*. *Tana nale* and *tana pad'du* are the homelands of the Indigenous Kodi people, it is one territory (*tana*) where the *nale* (savory seaworms) coexist with the *pad'du* (bitter substances), where the *wulla nale* ritual series that marks the abundance of the seaworm season—also known as the rainy season and the bland season—alternates with the *pad'du* ritual series that marks the scarcities of the dry season, which is the bitter season. This homeland is a place of abundance with densely concentrated, nutritious resources, like seaworms. The same place, though, is a land of starvation, with undesirable wild resources like bitter yams.

In the names *tana nale* and *tana pad'du* we see Kodi describing their identity through nature's rhythms and claiming their identity through their territory. As this chapter and the next chapter unfolds, a view of Kodi identity develops out of the discussions of people's relationships with seaworms.

"Land" (*tana* in Kodi; **banua* in Proto Malayo-Polynesian) is a key "organizing feature" (Fox 2006: 367) in Kodi as well as in many Austronesian societies, and indicates a genealogical tie between Austronesian languages. In Kodi, the concept of *tana nale* and the many discursive and nondiscursive associations with the "land of the seaworms" is a means by which people express human experiences and social identities.

Tana nale tana pad'du is a taxonomic mechanism for representing particular types of entities who inhabit Kodi worlds. *Tana nale tana pad'du* is a category of beings who choose to systematically shift their identities, and the category therefore also references a group of processes that are involved in identity shifting. The transtaxa beings who fit into the *tana nale tana pad'du* category inhabit a Kodi world where complementary dyads coexist within fluid fields. Kodi people identify with the alternating, cyclical, sequential, perpetuating rhythms of *tana nale tana pad'du* that they repeatedly experience in seasonality, seaworm biology, lunar periodicity, plant biology, and other consistent recurrences. In Kodi culture, the land is related to people, ancestor spirits, seaworms, the Moon, cultivated grains, wild yams, and to additional valorized figures because the processes through which these entities proceed through space-time is synchronous. These entities follow biosocial rhythms and are meaningfully included in the group of similar-but-different signalized beings. These entities belong in a league of their own: a transtaxa clade. The land, seasons, people, spirits, seaworms, the Moon, plants, etc. have heightened values in Kodi society as well as in numerous societies across the Austronesian and Papuan regions.

Within the group of transtaxa beings, seaworms have the very special quality of synchronizing their reproductive behaviors with other seaworms and with non-seaworm entities, both living and nonliving. Seaworms are a remarkably distinct group of social creatures who Kodi people most often encounter when people and seaworms converge on Sumba's tidal reefs, which are consummately translational fields (Ingold 2013). Tidal reefs are alternately flooded and drained twice per day, every day of the year, year after year. Tidal reefs alternate between landscape and seascape. Many of the creatures who live in tidal reefs are alternately accessible and inaccessible by humans because, when the tide recedes, people can walk onto the reefs. When the reef creatures are visible, people can reach down, pick them up, and put them in their containers. Or, in the case of the seaworms, the reef creatures are hidden or live elsewhere and are thus not available for most of the year regardless of the tides, and are available when other factors bring them en masse to the ocean surface above the reefs. Seaworms and people move together between landscapes and seascapes when the seaworms attract people to enter into their transitional marine environments and when people carry seaworms above the tidal zones to dry lands.

In their interactions with seaworms, Kodi people discursively and non-discursively express an emic conceptualization of the world as an animate cosmos. Their relationship with seaworms illustrates how Kodi people literally and figuratively construct their material and conceptual worlds by translating their experiences as members of multispecies communities into biosocial terms. These experiences are ones gained while moving through the biophysical landscape and while interacting with nonhuman species. To serve the purpose of chapters 2 and 3 to assess the cognition of biosocial change, I describe discursive and nondiscursive components of human life in tandem with seaworm biology taken from published reports about research on the reproductive biology and ecology of Polychaeta, the Class to which seaworms belong.

The evidence to evaluate human cognition of biosocial change comes from folk taxonomy (terms and their meanings) and embodied practices (rituals and movements). These sources of evidence contain people's expressions about their everyday and ritualized experiences with the phenomena of their worlds and their translations of those phenomena into biosocial constructs. The phenomena of most concern in chapters 2 and 3 are—to apply Smith's thoughts to this Polychaeta case (2013)[1]—the appearances of seaworms and the meanings seaworm appearances have in people's experiences. In focusing on these phenomena I attempt to represent the Kodi point of view and to also honor the agency of polychaetes, nonhuman humans, other types of nonhumans, and spirit humans. If I were capable, ideally I would adopt the polychaetes' point of view in order to represent "how [polychaetes] think," to paraphrase the title of Eduardo Kohn's book "How Forests Think: Toward an Anthropology Beyond the Human," but unfortunately I believe—because of my American-science-oriented worldview—the polychaetes' point of view is not knowable by me since I am a non-polychaete.

In the phenomenal island worlds of Eastern Indonesia, polychaetes are fully realized *selves* with "dispositions, motivations, and intentions" (Kohn 2007: 5). Anthropologists, marine biologists, naturalists, and others have noted the great cultural value people assign to polychaetes as long ago as 1702 when, upon visiting Ambon, Rumphius observed that *wawo* (Ambonese: polychaetes) were "a popular dish for the native population" (Horst 1902). More than 300 years later, polychaetes are still "highly prized foods" (Pawley and Green 1971: 121), a "much anticipated culinary delicacy," (Palmer and de Carvalho 2008: 1323), and people continue to swarm in ritual gatherings as they harvest from polychaete swarms (Pemungkas 2015). Polychaetes have powerful agency in Eastern Indonesia's oceans, in the landscape, in human culture, and in the spiritual realm. Humans facilitate polychaetes' agency in the domains of land, culture, and spirit, where polychaetes—together with many other phenomena—are the basis for the organization of space-time. Humans construct and organize space-time in particular ways as cultural responses to and correspondences with the allure of polychaetes' forms and behaviors, and polychaetes' relationships with other remarkable entities. I explore these proposals about the cognition of biosocial change by addressing several questions about the relationships between humans and polychaetes: What roles do polychaetes play in the ways people construct space-time? When and where do human expressions and movements reflect polychaetes' reproductive biology and ecology? By deeply contextualizing polychaetes in the space-time culture of Kodi, we find that the term "*nale* (polychaetes, seaworms, palolo)" refers to a category of beings who methodically switch taxonomic status and are thus transtaxa. What aspects of the whole biosocial context within which the human-polychaete relationships are enacted lead to the recognition of this (and other) creatures as being transtaxa?

The two-fold technique I use in this chapter and the next chapter to explore the many questions listed above about polychaete agency and the human cognition of *nale* in the context of biosocial change is to (1) perform a biosocial study and (2) perform a phenomenology of humans. Reconciling these two aims is challenging because biosocial studies would ideally represent nonhumans' point of view in a way that is not biased by humans, while phenomenology, like ethnography, was originally conceived as representing a specifically human world. Speculation to some extent is part of the endeavor to understand the world as nonhumans do, and anthropocentrism flavors the outcome. Science compensates for at least some human error, though, and empiricism partially compensates for our subjectivity. Evaluating human culture—one dimension of my treatment of human-polychaete interactions—relative to marine biology is an empirical exercise that can be approached using ethnographic methods to describe human beliefs and behaviors in combination with assessing information from scientific publications. Polychaete forms and behaviors are the qualities of seaworms that we humans can best access using our powers of observation since, while we can access human consciousness, we cannot yet access polychaetes' consciousness. Theory—which in tandem with empiricism is the basis for science—is key in this foray into biosocial studies because it provides a framework for interpreting polychaetes' behavior. Evolutionary theory of the kind Ingold (2013: 12) calls "the evolution of biosocial becomings" sets the stage for developing explanations in terms of polychaetes' reproductive biology and ecology. Ecological theory supports analyses of the relationships between biotic and abiotic factors, and how interactions within sea- and landscapes cause and effect change. Ethnobiological theory supports biosocial, phenomenological pursuits because it may lead writers to consider the ways ecological relationships affect human cognition and behavior. Empiricism and theory, evolution and ecology, marine biology, and ethnobiology are all part of the toolkit I use to craft this biosocial phenomenology.

A NARRATIVE FRAME FOR HISTORICAL PROCESS

Janet Hoskins, who conducted anthropological research in Kodi from 1979 to 1981 (and on several occasions thereafter) writes in *The Play of Time* that when she was trying to determine the best approach for studying Kodi culture a Kodi man told her, "If you don't know where to start . . . start with the sea worms [*sic*]. That is where we start ourselves" (Hoskins 1993: 80).

Hoskins interprets her friend's suggestion as an evaluation of time in Kodi culture because seaworms index the twelve-month ritual calendar (*Tanda Wulangu*) (Table 2.1). The tremendous significance of seaworms is apparent in Hoskins's summary of the connection between seaworms and the traditional Kodi calendar:

> The enumeration of month names was also an occasion for enumerating an annual round of social activities, the times of feasting and the times of famine, and also, I was to discover, the division of ceremonial tasks among ancestral villages and the location of objects that represent the historical process of acquiring these rights. The creation of the calendar at a consensus meeting of the ancestors provides the narrative frame that orients, to a certain extent, all Kodi storytelling about the past. All accounts of how crucial social institutions came into being are in some way related to the structure of the sea worm festivities and the divisions of the year. Knowledge of the calendar is focused on a few important ritual centers, invested in named religious officers (the *Rato Nale*, or "Priest of the Sea Worms"), and seen as something of a "native science." (Hoskins 1993: 80)

Based on her friend's suggestion, Hoskins produced the book *The Play of Time* about perceptions of time within their broader meaningful contexts.

Table 2.1   Kodi Lunar Calendar

Kodi Name for the Month	English Translation	Season
Wulla Nale Kiyo	Small Seaworms Month	Seaworm Season
Wulla Nale Bokolo	Big Seaworms Month	Harvest Season
Wulla Nale Walu	Last of the Seaworms Month	
Wulla Bali Mboka	Return of the *Mboka* (a type of flowering tree) Month	
Wulla Reno Kigya	Feast Preparation Month	Dry Season
Wulla Duka Reno	Feasting Month	
Wulla Katoto Lalo	*Katoto* (a type of flowering tree) Buds Month	
Wulla Katoto Bokolo	Big *Katoto* Month	
Wulla Paddu Laboya	Laboya Bitter Season Month	Bitter Season, Hungry Season
Wulla Paddu Kodi	Kodi Bitter Season Month	
Wulla Habbu	Nesting Month	
Wulla Mangata	*Mangata* (a type of mushroom) Month	

In this chapter of my own book, I also "start with the seaworms" and then embed them in the story of Kodi's biosocial network to identify the ways people connect their experiences with their identities, and link social change to ecological change.

POLYCHAETES IN MULTISPECIES SWARMS

Focusing on the topic of seaworms is an amazingly poetic means for ethnographically demonstrating that all humans on Earth live in multispecies worlds. I purposefully evoke Kirksey's "multispecies swarms" (Kirksey, n.d.) concept with my adoption of "swarms" as a key word here in this study of human-polychaete interactions. In Kirksey's vision for multispecies ethnography, "swarms" are political movements and tactical scholarly gatherings. Kirksey's term is perfectly suited for my own purposes too, and, moreover, has standard usage in biology. In the context of polychaete biology, marine ecology, and animal science, "swarms" are aggregates of similar organisms who intermingle in some location, or who move or migrate together. Swarming behaviors are seen in marine organisms, insects, birds, and herd animals. A few of the swarmers in the marine world in addition to polychaetes, are "barnacles, corals, sponges, ascidians, and echinoderms" (Sweeney et al. 2011: 770) who are most active at dusk, and thus belong to the vespertine class of crepuscular creatures. They swarm to spawn. We add humans to the list of organisms who display swarming behavior, as Kirksey does, and delve into the study of "assemblages of people and animals" (Kosek 2010 cited in Kirksey, n.d., under "Swarm"). Kirksey and other scholars (e.g., Kosek 2010; Thacker 2004) borrow a swarm model from biology and ecology and then apply it to social relationships in human groups and human-nonhuman networks. Swarms are touchstones for the literal and conceptual construction of space, time, and life in the space-time cultures of social scientists and marine biologists as well as among Kodi people.

Diverse cultures throughout the Indo-Pacific region experience a world where "multispecies swarms" (Pamungkas and Glasby 2015) of breeding polychaetes are ripe tropes for organizing society, identity, space, and time. As a group, polychaetes exhibit incredible morphological and behavioral diversity, and human interactions with polychaetes reflect this. Polychaetes converge into groups when they breed. When they are not breeding some polychaetes live as independent individuals while others practice commensalism or parasitism.

In those polychaete species that converge in swarms, humans recognize their spectacular morphology and behavior. The recognition of their splendidness is evident in Gaston and Hall's description of what glowworms

(*Odontosyllis luminosa* Syllidae San Martin 1990) do as the light of the waning gibbous Moon shines on Caribbean reefs:

> Female *O. luminosa* left the bottom and drifted slowly on surface currents where they periodically began luminescing. . . . Males could be seen flashing a pattern of luminescence on turtlegrass blades below the females, apparently in response to glowing of the females. Males left the bottom, flashing bioluminescence as they swam rapidly toward the surface to join the females. . . . Females began quivering rapidly and spinning in circles while releasing a luminescent mass and (presumably) gametes. Males swam rapidly around the females bioluminescing and releasing their gametes. Sometimes several males encircled a single female. Each luminescent episode lasted for 45–60 sec, but some female worms repeated the episodes numerous times as they drifted near the surface. Generally, once males were attracted, the spawning female lasted just 2–3 min. Some females apparently were not successful in attracting males and did not undergo the oocyte-releasing behavior. Rather they continued to emit their bioluminescent mass while drifting at the surface. (Gaston and Hall 2000: 47)

Assemblies of swimming, spinning, gamete-releasing polychaetes, like the ones Gaston and Hall describe, are referred to as "swarms." The polychaetes in the swarms are the fertile versions, or epitokes, of individuals who belong to the Polychaeta Class in the Annelida Phylum and who are spewing their eggs and sperm out onto the ocean's surface (World Conservation Monitoring Centre 1996). At least eighteen families in the Polychaeta Class swarm when they breed, including the Eunicidae, Nereididae, and Syllidae (Pemungkas and Glasby 2015). Some swarms contain representatives of multiple families and species. In the 1600s, Horst, a Dutch colonial resident of Eastern Indonesia, described the diversity in size and color of the polychaete swarms in Ambon's coastal waters as follows: ". . . green, yellow, and purple colored . . . from 8–40 cm in length and 2–3 mm wide" (Horst 1902, under "Over de Wawo"). Whether the Dutch colonists were seeing differently gendered and colored individuals in the same species of *Palola viridis* (Eunicidae Gray 1847), or different polychaete species is unknown, but numerous species have been found in other swarms around the world. In March 2014, Indonesian scientists found twenty-five distinct species representing five families in a swarm on Ambon's coast (Pemungkas 2015). In the waters near Lizard Island on Australia's Great Barrier Reef, surveyors collected fourteen genera and thirty-eight species or species groups belonging to the Nereididae Family alone, not to mention other families (Glasby and Fauchald 2007). In Caribbean swarms, scientists (Gaston and Hall 2000) found representatives from four Polychaeta clades: syllidae, nereidids, opheliids, and spionids. A diverse collection of other kinds of marine creatures—amphipods, isopods, tanaids, Atherinidae (the predator silversides, ill-fated because they die after eating the bioluminescent material in seaworms)—were swimming in the Caribbean swarms together with the polychaetes (Gaston and Hall 2000). In Florida's Keys, fishermen are attracted to the polychaete swarms not to catch the polychaetes themselves, but to catch the other game fish who come to feed from the swarms.

No similar surveys are available showing the number of species in swarms around Sumba's shorelines. Scientists aboard the Snellius II expedition in 1984 are among the few groups who have thus far collected polychaete specimens from the northeast coast of Sumba (Table 2.2), so scientific knowledge of the seaworms on Sumba is incomplete. We might hypothesize, though, that numerous species of polychaetes and also numerous other taxa compose multispecies swarms in Sumba's reefs.

POLYCHAETA DIVERSITY, RANGE, AND HABITAT

"Seaworms" is the common English term for a diverse collection of marine invertebrates and is the term most often used in ethnographic literature, though they are also known by the common English names "bristle worms," "palolo," and "polychaetes." The creatures that are in the common English category "seaworms" have until recently belonged to the Annelida Phylum which is made up of the three classes Polychaeta (marine worms), Oligochaeta (earthworms), and Hirudinea (leeches). However, recent taxonomic work raises questions about whether the Annelida Phylum, which currently contains 16,500 species, is one or multiple phylums. The polychaetes' range extends from the arctic to the temperate and tropical regions. The Polychaeta Class includes eighty-two families (Glasby and Fauchald 2007). Whether and which families belong to which higher-order taxa is under construction and debatable, so some scientists place them in clades while the taxonomy is being worked out (Australian Museum, n.d.). The Polychaeta Class has about 1000 genera and 13,000 species that have been identified thus far; potentially thousands more species likely exist, but have not yet been identified (Halanych, Cox, and Struck 2007). Seventy-eight taxa of polychaetes are known from the Indo-Pacific region (Glasby and Fauchald 2007).

Much work remains to be done on the taxonomy of polychaetes in marine biology as well as in ethnobiology. The Kodi term for seaworms, *nale*, has cognates in other western Sumbanese languages, but the Kodi term is not cognate to other Austronesian and Papuan languages, nor to languages with historical roots in the PCEMP (Proto Central-Eastern Malayo-Polynesian) and PAN (Proto Austronesian) categories. Studying the genealogy of the term *nale* could provide clues to the history of Sumbanese people, the settlement of the island by Austronesians and Papuans, and relationships between Austronesian and Papuans. A historical linguistic analysis of *nale*

Table 2.2   List of Seaworm Specimens Collected from Waters near Sumba*

Zootaxa	Collector, Site, Date	Citation
Branchiosyllis maculata Imajima 1966	Snellius II, NE coast of Sumba, 09°57'S 120°48'E, September 16, 1984	Aguado, Guillermo, and ten Hove 2008
Branchiosyllis verrculosa Augener 1913	Snellius II, NE coast of Sumba, 09°57'S 120°48'E, September 16, 1984	Aguado, Guillermo, and ten Hove 2008
Eusyllis assimilis Marenzeller 1875	Snellius II, NE coast of Sumba, 09°57'S 120°48'E, September 16, 1984	Aguado, Guillermo, and ten Hove 2008
Eusyllis lamelligera Marion and Bobretzky 1875	Snellius II, NE coast of Sumba, 09°57'S 120°49'E, September 16, 1984	Aguado, Guillermo, and ten Hove 2008
Haplosyllides sp.	Snellius II, NE coast of Sumba, 09°57'S 120°49'E, September 16, 1984	Aguado, Guillermo, and ten Hove 2008
Haplosyllides aberrans Fauvel 1939	unknown	WoRMs N.D.
Haplosyllis aciculata Lattig, Martin, and Aguado 2010	NE coast of Sumba, 09°57'S 120°49'E	Lattig, Martin, and Aguado 2010
Lygdamis ehlersi major Caullery 1944	unknown	
Marphysa soembaensis Augener 1933	unknown	Salazar-Vallejo et al. 2014; Read and Fauchald 2015
Neanthes pachychaeta Fauvel 1918	unknown	Fauvel 1918; Glasby, Wilson, and Bakken 2011
Odontosyllis freycinetensis Augener 1913	Snellius II, NE coast of Sumba, 09°57'S 120°48'E, September 16, 1984	Aguado, Guillermo, and ten Hove 2008
Opisthopista sibogae Caullery 1944	unknown	Caullery 1944
Pionosyllis sp. Malmgren 1867	Snellius II, NE coast of Sumba, 09°57'S 120°49'E, September 16, 1984	Aguado, Guillermo, and ten Hove 2008
Spiraserpula deltoides Serpulidae Pillai and ten Hove 1994	Pillai and ten Hove, Sumba	Read and Fauchald 2015; ten Hove and Kupriyanova 2009
Spiraserpula sumbensis Serpulidae Pillai and ten Hove 1994	Pillai and ten Hove, Sumba	Read and Fauchald 2015; ten Hove and Kupriyanova 2009
Syllis ypsiloides n. sp.	Snellius II, NE coast of Sumba, 09°57'S 120°49'E, September 16, 1984	Aguado, Guillermo, and ten Hove 2008
Syllis sp.	Snellius II, NE coast of Sumba, 09°57'S 120°49'E, September 16, 1984	Aguado, Guillermo, and ten Hove 2008

* This list is incomplete. Some of the polychaetes that have already been collected from the waters near Sumba have not yet been identified, and some polychaete families that are suspected to occur in the area have not yet been collected or identified (Christopher Glasby, email communication 2016)

could support attempts to determine whether or not Sumba was first settled by Papuan populations prior to the arrival of Austronesian settlers as human genetic data suggests (Lansing et al. 2007).

Polychaetes inhabit benthic and pelagic water zones; salt, brackish, or fresh water zones; oceans, estuaries, lakes and rivers; mud and sand; hydrothermal vents and cold seeps (Glasby and Fauchald 2007; Read and Fauchald 2015). Polychaetes "are one of the most commonly encountered and abundant animal groups in the benthos of coastal regions" (Glasby and Fauchald 2007, under "What are Polychaetes"). Depending on the species, polychaetes spend most of their lives on the sea floors either wandering around the floor, burrowing or nestling into the substrate, or living in tubes; or most of their lives swimming around in the pelagic zones; or, for the evolutionarily transitional species, their time is divided between bottom-dwelling in the benthic zones and free-swimming in the pelagic zones. Polychaetes are found in coral reefs, fore-reefs, back-reefs, reef slopes, tide pools, seagrass beds, lagoons, and mangroves.

The Polychaeta Class is divided into the Subclass Sedentaria, whose members are tube dwellers, and the Subclass Errantia, whose members are free swimmers. Some of the diagnostic features of polychaetes are segmentation, parapodia (flat outgrowths), chaetae/setae (small, moveable bristles, and the source of the name "Polychaeta" meaning "many bristles"), and tube construction. Head morphology is another diagnostic feature with the character of the antenna and the palps—which are sensors—serving to identify species. Because polychaetes are so diverse, however, many taxa do not display diagnostic features, and have modified or no segmentation, no parapodia, or no chaetae, and many do not produce tubes. Some polychaete species are as long as three meters (ten feet) and some species are as short as 0.1 mm (0.004 inches).

SYNCHRONIZED CYCLES

Diverse marine taxa synchronize their breeding behaviors to maximize reproductive success. Combined external and internal mechanisms prompt marine taxa to swarm and thus coproduce the temporality of spawning. Mercier and Hamel (2015: 107) list "temperature . . . lunar irradiance . . . lunar photoperiod . . . tidal levels . . . seasonal photoperiod . . . and twilight chromaticity" (Mercier and Hamel 2015) as the thus far documented external circadian and circalunar mechanisms associated with mass spawning. Among the internal mechanisms that regulate polychaete spawning is the endocrine system (Australian Museum, n.d.; Wu 2014). Most types of polychaetes are vespertine who congregate on coral reefs in multispecies swarms to spawn at twilight during the waning gibbous Moon.

Like scientists, Kodi recognize the effect of the Moon on the reproductive biology of polychaetes. Among other things, the Moon signifies to the *Rato Nale* (Seaworm Priests) when the seaworms will swarm. Both scientists and Kodi observe that polychaetes begin swarming at dusk on the nights after full Moons. The full Moon of the Return of Seaworm Month in the Kodi calendar marks the start of the counting of nights until the time when Kodi people make their seaworm pilgrimage to the region's reefs. The exact number of nights after the full Moon when seaworms swarm remains a question the Seaworm Priests are tasked with predicting each year.

EXTERNAL MECHANISMS TO CUE SPAWNING

The synchronization of the seaworm swarming times is complexly constituted. Among the ideas about the determinants of the swarming time of the day is circadian rhythms, the swarming days of the month is circalunar cycles, and the months of the year is seawater temperature variations (Mercier and Hammel 2015). Some scientists propose that circadian cycles are a stronger cue for spawning than circalunar cycles (Sweeney et al. 2011) though they work in tandem. Members of the Syllidae Family (specifically, *Odontosyllis luminosa* and *O. enopla*) of polychaetes in the Caribbean,[2] for example, mostly swarm between fifty and seventy minutes after sunset (Gaston and Hall 2000; Scott and Wood, n.d.), when the waning Moon is slightly below or right on the horizon (Sweeney et al. 2011). Circadian and circalunar cycles together have greater impact on the periodicity of swarming behavior than does cloud cover, wind, or tide level in *O. luminosa* and possibly other polychaetes as well (Gaston and Hall 2000; Scott and Wood, n.d.). Tide levels may affect swarming times in some locations and some species (Endres and Schad 2002). Because mass spawning behaviors correlate with shifts in the intensities and wavelengths of light that co-occur with changes in the Moon's phase and elevation relative to the horizon (Sweeney et al. 2011), marine biologists propose that mass, synchronous free-spawning may have "evolved in response to lunar-mediated spectral variations" (Sweeney et al. 2011: 770).

Causal pathways in biosocial networks are immensely complex, though, so synchrony is very complex. The Moon is an ecosystem engineer in the marine environment via its influences on tidal processes, spectral dynamics, and via numerous linked pathways. Tide levels systematically vary during the course of the Moon's 18.6-year-long oscillation of declination, which affects submersion and emersion periodicity in intertidal ecosystems. The amount of time an intertidal ecosystem is submersed or emersed impacts the abundance and distribution of primary producers. An example is the canopy-cover kelp *Saccharina sessilis*, which is itself an ecosystem engineer, a keystone species,

and a food resource for other organisms. The effects of tidal fluctuations on
S. sessilis has cascading effects in food web ecologies (Burnaford, Nielsen,
and Williams 2014). The researchers who discovered the connection between
the Moon and *S. sessilis* were working in the intertidal zones of San Juan
Island in Washington state in the United States, so this example does not
illustrate the coupling of lunar, tidal, botanical, and zoological processes in
Sumba's intertidal zones, but I cite the study here to suggest that the Moon
affects Earth's ecosystems, including Sumba's coral reef ecosystems, in
myriad ways.

Twilight spectral dynamics is a key component of the circadian cycle that
cues multispecies swarms on coral reefs (Sweeney et al. 2011). Dusk is a
period of shifting intensities and wavelengths in light during the transition
from sunlight to moonlight (Huntsman 1948; Sweeney et al. 2011). In the
transition from light/day to dark/night, the spectrum is a "varying mixture of
blue-shifted sunlight and the slightly red-shifted moonlight" (Sweeney et al.
2011: 773), and the mixture changes each night depending on the Moon's elevation. Kodi people perceive the light of the full Moon as being red (*taru rara*)
(Hoskins 1993), which is similar to the scientific understanding of moonlight.
"Moonlight is red shifted compared with daylight," write Sweeney et al.
(2011: 770).

The aspect of the circalunar cycle that coproduces lunar periodicity[3] in
polychaetes is the altitude of the Moon at twilight. The influence of moonlight on twilight varies over the course of the Moon's phases, depending on
whether the Moon is above the horizon during the waxing phases, on the
l   on during the full Moon, or below the horizon during the waning phases.
Th. ectrum changes in the shift from Sun-dominated light before the Sun
sets, to a transition stage after the Sun sets and before the Moon rises, and
then to Moon-dominated light after the Moon rises. The timing of the shift
differs each night because the Moon's rise relative to the Sun's setting gets
about fifty minutes later each night after the full Moon. Before the full Moon,
when the Moon rises before the Sun sets, the shift in hue and colorfulness
(i.e., chromaticity) in sunlight to moonlight happens faster than after the full
Moon when the Moon rises after the Sun sets. The mass spawners enjoy the
longer lag times in the shift from Sun-dominated chromaticity to Moon-
dominated chromaticity.

Among corals that spawn during twilight in Caribbean reefs, to give an
example, their visual systems are able to detect color differences, especially
in ambient chromaticity, between the waxing gibbous Moon in the days just
prior to the full Moon and the waning gibbous Moon in the days just after the
full Moon even though the Moon is at −10° solar elevation at both of those
times (Sweeney et al. 2011). Moreover, within a single night, the corals are
so perceptive of the shifting ambient skylight that they use it to cue the stages

in the spawning process by setting bundles ("when gamete bundles are moved out of the gonads and into the gastric cavity of coral polyps and spawning is inevitable" [Sweeney et al. 2011: 774]) in the blue-shifted twilight very soon after the Sun sets, and then releasing gametes into the open water once the light shifts to the Moon-dominated spectra (Sweeney et al. 2011).

Coral species' visual systems require some type of photoreceptors to sense the light, but do not require eyes. In the Polychaeta class, many species do have eyes. The spawning epitokes of some polychaete species, such as *Palola viridis*, which occur in Eastern Indonesia, have eye spots to sense light and help them navigate through the ocean. Their eye spots "consist of a round- to oval-shaped pigment spot and a central cuticular lense" (Schulze and Timm 2012: 162).

INTERNAL MECHANISMS TO CUE SPAWNING

The methods through which polychaetes breed vary depending on the species. Most polychaetes reproduce sexually, other species are hermaphrodites that have both female and male sexual capabilities, some switch sexes from male to female during the course of their lives, and others reproduce asexually. Some species of polychaetes breed only one day in their lives, but others breed multiple times during their lifespan.

The polychaete species that reproduce sexually in broadcast spawning events undergo bodily transformations before releasing their gametes in the water through morphological transformations, epitoky, or stolonization. Epitoky—the production of epitokes for the purpose of swimming and reproducing—involves several morphological transformations that cause the worms to shift from nonreproductive into reproductive individuals. The initiation of epitoky by hormones causes the synchronization of male and female breeding times, and leads males and females to spawn at the same time. Female pheromones stimulate males to release sperm which in turn causes females to release eggs. The morphological changes that occur during epitoky include becoming bioluminescent about one month prior to spawning (Daly 1975; Wilkens and Wolken 1981), developing paddle-like chaetae, pigment changes (Fischer and Fischer 1995), degeneration of the digestive system, and the production of eggs and sperm. Some polychaete species produce epitokes through epigamy when they detach their atokes (anterior sections) from their epitokes (posterior sections) and produce sperm or eggs in their epitokes. Some sedentary polychaete species create epitokes through schizogamy by budding when they sprout stolon-like epitokes from their posteriors or polypodias that detach and swarm. Stonolonization—not the most common method of reproduction in polychaetes—is practiced by *Syllinae*, a Subfamily with at least two representatives on Sumba: *Haplosyllides aberrans* (Fauvel 1939) and *Haplosyllis aciculata* (Lattig, Martin, and Aguado 2010).

The epitokes use their parapodia and chaetae (some are shaped like paddles) to swim, sometimes in groups, to the ocean surface where they join swarms of other epitokes.

Some polychaetes are bioluminescent, and nerves control the release of light via luminescent secretions or slimes. Females of some species release light from photocells to attract the luminescent males. Light attracts the polychaetes, a trait that their human predators exploit by using torches and flashlights to pull the polychaetes to the ocean surface and into their nets.

The stolons of many species, including *Syllinae*, die after they release their eggs or sperm, possibly because their digestive organs degenerate to clear space for the eggs and sperm. The parents of the stolons, however, survive on the ocean floor and may produce additional stolons in the future. If they survive the swarming events, those species that produce epitokes by transforming their entire bodies into reproductive forms can transform back into their prior form, by shedding their swimming chaetae, regaining their pigment, and returning to the bottom where they build new tubes and become sedentary again. The fertilized eggs develop into trochophore larvae and later into adult polychaetes.

CORRESPONDING SWARMS OF POLYCHAETES AND PEOPLE

Variations in the "annual, seasonal, monthly, and daily" cycles (Sweeney et al. 2011: 770) of polychaete spawning occur across space and even in the same space across time. The variations may depend on the Moon's phase, day length, seawater temperature, solar radiation, light:dark cycles, photosynthates from zooxanthellae, and cryptochrome cycles (Sweeney et al. 2011). Polychaete spawning varies depending on location (Table 2.3). In some locations, polychaetes swarm numerous times within annual, seasonal, and monthly intervals. In eastern Oceania, one of the most common and most well-known polychaetes, *P. viridis*, breeds on the "second or third day after the third quarter of the Moon in October or November" (World Conservation Monitoring Centre 1996, under "Habitat and Ecology"). In other locations and for certain species, polychaetes swarm throughout the year. Caribbean Syllidae swarm on the first three nights after the full Moon during every month of the year (Gaston and Hall 2000; Scott and Wood, n.d.). Scientists who study the reproductive biology of seaworms in the Caribbean find polychaetes swarming three and four nights after the full Moon. The bioluminescing *O. luminosa*[4] in the Caribbean lagoons and fore-reefs off the coast of Belize swarm year round with peaks during June, July, and August (Gaston and Hall 2000: 47).

In Eastern Indonesia, Rumphius' acquaintances on Ambon in 1702 told him, "We do not see the *wawo* (Ambonese: polychaetes) throughout the whole year. Only on the second and third and fourth evenings after the full Moons of February and March do we see them after sunset swimming on the water near the beaches where large rocks full of cracks are" (Horst 1902).

Rumphius followed up on this information by verifying that he saw polychaetes swarming in Ambon's coastal waters in 1684 on March 3, 4, and 5 following the full Moon on March 1, and also in 1685 on March 22 and 23 following the full Moon on March 20. Rumphius made similar observations in 1686, 1687, 1688, 1690, 1693, and 1694. In the 1700s in Ambon, local people held seaworm gathering festivals on "a few specific days" (Horst 1902) to coordinate with the days the polychaetes swarmed.

Rumphius's Ambonese acquaintances very well may have guided Rumphius to see the swarming seaworms on those nights during those waning Moons, but his accounts from Ambon in the 1600s and the continuing practices on Sumba suggest that human swarming behaviors for ritualized harvests *correspond* to nonhuman polychaete biology as well as other synchronized biosocial phenomena. Kodi say the swarming occurs six or seven nights after the full Moon, and that is when the ritual gatherings take place in Kodi. In 1998, the maximum illumination of the Moon was on March 13 and the ritual seaworm harvest took place seven days later on March 20 at Halete Beach. The Moon was twenty-two days old, in its waning gibbous phase, and 59 percent of the half facing Earth was illuminated. Compare this with the 2006 ritualized *Mechi Boot* "mass harvest of sea worms" (Palmer and de Carvalho 2008: 1322–1323) in the Tutuala subdistrict of East Timor's northern coast where the harvest took place at Velu beach on March 19–20, two days after the full Moon of March 15, 2006.

Swarms of *P. viridis* and other species rise to the surface in February and March in Eastern Indonesia and in October, November, and December in Oceania (Table 2.3). In Samoa, the local knowledge (which differs from the two to three night interval given by the World Conservation Monitoring Center) is that the seaworms swarm seven nights after the full Moon in the months of October and November; the number of nights after the full Moon is similar to Kodi, but the months of the year differ from Kodi. In Pago Pago, Samoa in 2009, *P. viridis* swarmed on November 8 and 9, 2009 which was five nights after the full Moon on November 3, 2009 (Schulze and Timm 2012). The seaworm gathering tradition has a long history in Samoa as attested to by early European visitors like John B. Stair who in 1897 wrote that seaworms are "held in such universal esteem as to be considered a national luxury" (Stair 1897).

A synchronic aspect of polychaete breeding is in annual variations in the size of swarms. Rumphius, for example, noted that the amounts of seaworms

Table 2.3 The Months and Location of Seaworm Swarming and Local Seaworm Rituals in the Indo-Pacific Region

Seaworm Species	Swarming Times	Swarming Location	Seaworm Ritual	Swarming Rhythm
Lumbriconereis sphaerocephlae Eunicidae	Last quarter	Vanuatu	Unknown	
Lumbriconereis sp. Eunicidae	"second and third night after Full Moon in March and April"*	Moluccas	Unknown	Lunar
Lysidice fallax Eunicidae	"last quarter of the Moon in October about 1–2 days before palolo"*	Samoa	Yes	Lunar and annual
Lysidice oele Horst Eunicidae	Twilight; "on second, third, and fourth day after Full Moon in February, March, and April"*	Ambon, Moluccas	Yes	Diurnal, lunar, annual
Nematonereis sp. Eunicidae	"second and third night after Full Moon in March and April"*	Moluccas	Yes, in Ambon	Lunar and annual
Palola viridis (synonym Eunice viridis) Eunicidae	Before sunrise; October, November, December; last quarter	South Pacific: Samoa, Kiribati, Tonga, Fiji, Vanuatu, etc.	Yes, in Samoa	Diurnal, lunar, annual
Palola viridis Eunicidae	March, April	Ambon	Yes, in Ambon	
Unknown, possibly Palola viridis	February, March	Sumba	Yes, in Kodi	
Odontosyllis hyaline Grube Phyllodocidae	Twilight; 3 nights after Full Moon*	Jakarta	Unknown	Lunar and diurnal

* Endres and Schad 1997: 171–174

on Ambon's coast in the ten years between 1684 and 1694 varied from "no seaworms" on March 1, 1687 to "many seaworms" from March 21–27, 1693.

Perhaps because they coincide with the swarming times of seaworms, variations exist in the timing of seaworm rituals across the Indo-Pacific (Table 2.3). Among the numerous islands whose inhabitants perform rituals when seaworms swarm are Sumba, Lombok (Eklund 1977), Sumbawa (Welker 2009), Ambon (Pemungkas and Glasby 2015), East Timor (McWilliam 2006; Palmer and de Carvalho 2008), Savu, Roti, Fiji, Gilbert Islands, Tonga, Samoa, and elsewhere in the Eastern Pacific (Kirch and Green 2001). In western Sumba, East Timor, and Ambon people perform seaworm rituals in January, February, March, and/or April (Horst 1902; McWilliam 2006; Palmer and de Carvalho 2008; Pemungkas and Glasby 2015; Radjawane 1982).

Like the Kodi community on Sumba, the Fataluku community in East Timor performs seaworm harvests twice per year during the waning phases of the Moon: first is the *Mechi Kiik* (Small Seaworms) in February and second is *Mechi Boot* (Large Seaworms) in March. The harvests take place at several locations, including Velu beach (Palmer and de Carvalho 2008) and Telu'o beach, where the Fataluku ancestors came ashore when they discovered the island (McWilliam 2006).

Communities who live in the western Central Pacific perform seaworm rituals in October or November. Residents of Vanuatu's Torres Islands, for example, ritually mark the October swarming of seaworms (Mondragon 2004). Fijians perform four-day-long seaworm festivals. Futunans observe the seaworm swarm in September, October, and November.

The ritualized link across the borders of land and ocean provides evidence that communities throughout the Indo-Pacific perceive seaworm swarms, crop agronomy, lunar periodicity, seasonal wet-dry alternations, and other cyclical processes as being interlinked. These interlinkages produce biosocial patterns. Moreover, people in these communities translate the patterns they perceive in biosocial rhythms into annual ritual calendars (Condominas 1977). In doing so, they mold their identities, in part, around their relationships with the other entities with whom their cycles synchronize.

NOTES

1. Smith (2013) defines the meaning of the term phenomena for phenomenologists as, "the appearances of things, or things as they appear in our experience, or the ways we experience things, thus the meanings things have in our experience" (Smith 2013, under "What is Phenomenology?").

2. Syllidae species occur in the waters off of Sumba's coast. The Snellius II expedition collected the Syllidae representative *Odontosyllis freycinetensis* (Augener

1913) from the northeastern coast of Sumba on September 16, 1984. Worldwide, 52 species of *Odontosyllis* occur (Read and Fauchald 2015).

3. Lunar periodicity means, "a biological rhythm . . . [in which] the maxima and minima of the rhythmical process appear once or twice in every lunar month at the same time, that is, at the time of a certain moon phase" (Hauenschild 1960: 491).

4. A bioluminescent species known to inhabit Indonesian waters is *Odontosyllis hyalina* (Syllidae Grube 1978) (Gaston and Hall 2011).

Chapter 3

The Interchangeability of Humans, Seaworms, and Spirits

Kodi people perceive the world as one where human humans, dead humans, supernatural nonhumans, and other nonhumans metamorphose at particular times and in particular places into one another (cf. Viveiros de Castro 2014). These are transtaxa figures who have the ability to cross the boundaries of taxa, and/or to simultaneously occupy more than one taxa. Whatever form they take at any particular time or location is a periodic yet ephemeral "coherence situated amid ever-transforming divisions and connections" (Yates-Doerr 2015: 309). The transtaxa beings are male, female, or both; they are one, two, or more than two species; they inhabit the world of the dead, the world of the living, or go back and forth between these; they are deities and ancestors. Numerous transtaxa figures populate the *Marapu* pantheon of deities, spirits, and ancestors. Mother Seaworm is one of these transtaxa figures. She swings gracefully over the boundaries of the seaworm, spirit, and ancestor taxa. She easily crosses the boundaries between near shore and deep water, ocean and land, atmosphere and ground. Mother Seaworm traverses the borders between life and death, repeatedly and at will. Other spirits are transtaxa too, including Biri Koni and Ra Hapu whose stories appear below. The apical ancestors of the major patriclans in Kodi are transtaxa characters: Grandfather Python is the forefather for patriclans in the villages of Tossi, Bukubani, Wei Yeŋgho, and Karendi; Grandfather Lobster is the apical ancestor for another patriclan in Bukubani; Grandfather Rat for a patriclan in Karendi; Grandfather Goat for the Mete patriclan; and Grandfather Crocodile for the Rato Ngaro patriclan. The figures in this list are the progenitors of living Kodi people.

Many humans in Kodi think of their ancestors as being part human and part nonhuman, and of themselves as being related through kinship to nonhuman creatures. The apical ancestors are all taxa-crossing creatures: the clan origin myths tell stories about when the apical ancestors, who were originally nonhumans, transformed into humans in order to procreate with human women. A collection of other stories tell about characters who crossed the species barriers in the other direction. These characters started their lives out as humans and transformed into nonhumans. Other characters made the crossing because they suffered violent deaths; such as Biri Koni, who crossed taxa when her father sacrificed her, and Mother Seaworm, who crossed taxa after she sacrificed herself. Mother Seaworm's myth that explains the origins of seaworms and Biri Koni's myth that explains the origins of cultivated plants are written below. Upon dying, Biri Koni, Mother Seaworm, and all of the patriarchs who beget patriclans crossed taxa again: they transformed from living humans to dead humans, also known as *marapu* (ancestors), who continue to live in the same world as living humans but who have additional abilities for navigating through and affecting changes in the parts of the cosmos that are inaccessible to living humans. In this chapter, you will read what happens to the spirits of contemporary living plants, animals, and humans when they suffer violent deaths like Biri Koni and Mother Seaworm, and also when they die in their old age.

Kodi speakers pass along information about human pasts and futures as transtaxa beings, and about other taxa-crossing beings in everyday conversations and in formal storytelling situations. When narrating their mythologies, Kodi storytellers de-center humans as they locate the cosmos's beings in time and space relative to one another. In the temporal dimension, storytellers locate transspecies as predecessors and/or successors to humans. In the space dimension, Kodi locate living humans, dead humans, and nonhumans relative to the landscape. Stories about the dead humans who are the ancestors of living Kodi people are recounted in a collection of myths that represent the classical Indo-Australian genre of legends retracing the ancestors' footprints (Fowler 2013; Tamisari 1998). As goes for the Kodi in Eastern Indonesia, so also goes for the Walbiri and the Yolngu in Australia: the ancestors' footprints take "spatial forms" (Munn 1973) that materialize in places that are sacred, governed by taboos, and visited for rituals. Found cross-culturally in the Indo-Australian region, the places where the ancestors left their footprints are, "ritually defined, ceremonially ordered social space" (Fox 2006: 371). Many examples are available from throughout the region.

One prototypical example of a story about an ancestor's footprints from Kodi is the story of *Limmo Manu*, one of the places where the seaworms swarm. In the old days, Kodi used to gather seaworms at *Limmo Manu*, but now they gather seaworms elsewhere. The ancestors' exploits in this sacred place are memorialized in the following seaworm origins myth.

> In the old days, the Kings of Sumba's rival ethnic groups went to war frequently.
> In one of the legendary battles, two Kings fought over the hand of a woman who

they both loved. She was the beautiful daughter of the nobleman-priest, Rato Ndimya. Rato Ndimya's daughter loved both of the Kings and could not decide herself which one she would marry. To determine who would get her hand, the elders told the two Kings that they must go to battle at the rocky ocean cliff named *Limmo Manu*.

When Rato Ndimya's daughter heard of the battle she rushed to *Limmo Manu* to stop the fighting. She stood between the two Kings, and grabbed their hands in hers.

"Do not go to war because of me," said Rato Ndimya's daughter. "Because you fight like this, neither one of you can have me!"

She let loose of the two Kings' hands, and threw herself off of the high cliff into the rocky ocean far below. Upon reaching the ocean waters, her body transformed into seaworms. She was immortalized in the figure of a goddess whose name is *Inya Nale* (Mother Seaworm).

The human manifestation of Mother Seaworm was the daughter of the ancient nobleman-priest Rato Ndimya. Rato Ndimya's daughter was the key item in an exchange between the Wife Giver Rato Ndimya and the Wife Taker Lendu, who represents all Earthbound Kodi people. In giving his daughter to Lendu, Rato Ndimya was conferring a "gift of returning life, to renew the land with fresh waters" (Hoskins 1993: 89). The marriage exchange went awry, however, because Rato Ndimya's daughter had more than one suitor. Both suitors were Kings and their desire for Rato Ndimya's daughter led them to declare war. The rivalry between the two suitors was devastating for Rato Ndimya's daughter, and the seaworm myth explains the outcome of the competition for her hand.

The seaworm origin myth tells a story about an event that occurred in the mythological past when a human simultaneously crossed the ocean-land borderline and the Mammalia-Polychaeta boundary. Nowadays, seaworms manifest as nonhuman seaworms, or as a spirit human. The form she takes at any given moment synchronizes with the Moon's phase, the seasonal cycle, plant biology, agropastoral activities, and the annual ritual and social calendar. The seaworm origin tale is also about social status since it is a story about members of an elite, royal class, and reveals the hierarchical character of the Austronesian-Papuan society. The seaworm myth teaches people how humans relate to their companions with whom they coexist in this world. Other instances in Kodi mythology do parallel world-making work, including the Biri Koni story, which describes a cosmos in which human humans and transtaxa beings coproduce one another's bodies and souls. The wise elders who narrate the seaworm origins myth promise Kodi people that, when they follow ritual protocol to consume seaworms, Mother Seaworm "will bring you fertility and the birth of new generations" (Hoskins 1993: 89).

Kodi people apprehend a reality where spirits appear in the living world just as living beings cross into the spiritual realm. Mother Seaworm is one example, and another example is Biri Koni whose name is often translated in Indonesian as *Dewa Padi* (Rice Goddess), though she actually expresses characteristics of several key crops. We can think of Biri Koni as one multispecies, transtaxa being, or as a whole multispecies community in one figure. Biri Koni combines attributes of spirits, humans, rice, maize, cassava, leafy greens, and other flora as illustrated in the myth about the ancient Kodi couple, Lord Myabok and Lady Keŋgor, whose little girl, Biri Koni, transformed into the first domesticated crops. In the following version[1] of the Biri Koni myth, the girl's body parts are linked to the plant species to which they bear resemblances.

In the beginning, humankind on Earth and humankind up Above were in direct contact. Humans on Earth could travel back and forth using the *kawongo* tree (*Hibiscus tiliaceus* L. Malvaceae) as their path. Humankind on Earth hunted and gathered wild foods and subsisted on roots from the dirt and fruits from the trees. Earth people had no real "food"[2] [i.e., domesticated plants or animals]. Only humankind up Above had real food. Earth humans enjoyed eating real food with their relations when they visited them up Above. But the people up Above would not let Earth people bring food back to their homes on Earth.[3]

Lord Myabok and the few other men who lived in Kodi back then formed a delegation to make a formal request for real food from the people Above. They ascended the *kawongo* tree and begged the people Above to let them have real food on Earth. The people Above told Lord Myabok and his companions that if people on Earth wanted food, then they would have to make a gigantic sacrifice. They would have to kill Lord Myabok's daughter, Biri Koni, and build a gravestone for her in the middle of a forest clearing. The people Above forbid Lord Myabok to reveal his plan to his wife, Lady Keŋgor. They warned that, if Lord Myabok did tell Lady Keŋgor, then the great sacrifice would be futile because Biri Koni's body would not transform into food.

Lord Myabok and his companions decided to accept the bargain they were offered by the people Above. They would exchange an Earth child for real food. Lord Myabok began preparations to receive the food that the people Above would provide. He created a clearing in the forest by felling trees and slashing brush. Then, he burned the slash, and turned the soil with a hoe.

Lady Keŋgor came out to see what her husband was doing. She admired the hard work he did to clear the patch of forest. She was very proud of her husband's plan to bring real food to Earth.

Lady Keŋgor said, "What a wonderful idea to grow food! But what will you plant? Where will you get seeds?"

Lord Myabok replied, "I have a plan, dear Wife. Send our daughter Biri Koni to the garden."

While he was waiting for Lady Keŋgor to return with Biri Koni, Lord Myabok built a *Palondo Wini* (Seat of the Seeds altar) in the middle of the clearing (Photo 3.1).

When Lady Keŋgor arrived with Biri Koni, the father put the little girl on top of the bamboo platform that forms the base of the altar. This *Palondo Wini* was

Photo 3.1   Palondo Wini (Seat of the Seeds Altar) Surrounded by the Elder Woman Who is the Ritual Officiant and Her Family

be the girl's grave in the middle of the garden. He told his wife to return home and leave him and his daughter alone.

Lord Myabok then beheaded his daughter, cut her body up into pieces, and buried her body parts throughout the clearing.

Then he waited, trusting that the people Above would deliver on their end of bargain. After four long nights, plants began to sprout throughout his garden. This was the first garden in Kodi. The seedlings were bright green and grew very big. Biri Koni's big white eyes grew into Job's tears. Her teeth formed into maize kernels. Her lower legs developed into cassava. Leafy greens grew from her hair. Red sorghum sprouted from her blood. Her mother's milk that had filled Biri Koni's stomach turned into rice.[4]

Meanwhile, Lady Keŋgor continuously asked her husband, "Where is my daughter?"

But the husband did not have an answer for her. He would not tell her about the sacrificial killing of their child. Lady Keŋgor was heartsick because her daughter was missing. She went into mourning, meaning she stayed home, did not go out to work or to visit her neighbors. She forbid anyone to bang the gongs or beat the drums. Her sorrow was debilitating.

Eventually Lady Keŋgor left the house for the purpose of searching for Biri Koni. She searched in the grasslands, at the river's edge, and in the forests. On her way back home she passed by the garden that her husband created.

When she reached the edge of the garden Lady Keŋgor called out, "Come here Koni! Biri Koni! Where are you Koni?"

Biri Koni could hear her mother calling because the girl was actually still living, but in the form of crops.

Biri Koni answered, "Here I am, mother! I'm here!"

Lady Keŋgor could hear Biri Koni's reply, but she could not see her little girl. No little girl appeared in the garden. Only the newly acquired garden plants.

Lady Keŋgor called out again, "Where are you, Koni?! Come here, Koni!"

Again Biri Koni said, "I'm here! Here in the garden!" The little girl's voice was coming from the plants. "Look mother, I'm here!"

Lady Keŋgor looked all around the garden for her daughter, but she never found her. Lady Keŋgor is still there today circling the garden day and night. As she circles the garden looking for her daughter she protects the crops from being harmed by pests, theft, diseases, and fire.

A TRANSTAXA CATEGORY

Biri Koni is a transtaxa being: she is part plant, part human, part spirit. Mother Seaworm is a transtaxa being: she is part animal, part human, part spirit. These two figures fit into a category of transtaxa beings. These spiritual beings are "the same," according to a Kodi person. Garden crops and ocean foods are the same in the sense of both possessing souls, both provisioning living humans, both souls formerly being humans, both are still related to humans. More than that: the soul of the land-based garden belongs to the "same" biosocial community as the soul in the ocean-based garden, which is the "same" biosocial community as living humans and formerly living humans.

Biri Koni and Mother Seaworm are "same" also in the sense of being metaphors for one another. Both figures are female providers who sacrificed their own bodies in exchange for food. They were humans who sacrificed their bodies to obtain food. Their human bodies died, but their souls persist in living nonhuman bodies and in relationships with multispecies. Both souls formerly inhabited human bodies and now inhabit nonhuman bodies: plant bodies in Biri Koni's case and animal bodies in Mother Seaworm's case. These three types of bodies—plant, animal, human—house souls. When viewed through the analytical tool of seaworms, a single higher-order, transspecies category contains plants, animals, and humans. Beings in this category are transposable, they shift forms into one another's types of bodies, they swap substances, and therefore *correspond* (to use Ingold's term from 2013: 15) to one another.

The gender of the deities who are transspecies varies. Biri Koni and Mother Seaworm are both female symbols of sustenance and reproduction. The Mother Seaworm represents fertile marine animal life. Biri Koni represents fertile plant life. They similarly act as law enforcers, judges, and penalizers. In their many roles, the female spirits bare their connections with what mainstream, conventional European and American cultures often refer to as the "natural" world. The spirits' essences, bodies, emotions, and actions are interconnected with plants, animals, marine biology, agronomy, meteorology, geology, astronomy, and people too of course. Kodi recognize the interconnectedness of all of these components of their world. In the Kodi worldview, these two female spirits facilitate seaworm reproduction, plant reproduction, and human sustenance for the purpose of supporting human wellbeing at a level that promotes moral conduct and prevents natural disasters.

While Biri Koni and Mother Seaworm are female, other transspecies beings exhibit other genders. One group of transspecies deities is male: the ancient python-human, lobster-human, crocodile-human, rat-human, and goat-human who were the founders of patriclans. Another group of deities is double gendered: Great Mother Great Father, Mother Guardian of the Land Father Guardian of the Rivers, Mother Seaworm Father Fish. "Double gendered" is Hoskins's (1990) term for describing the gender of a group of Kodi deities whose names include terms for both males and females. The deities *Inya Mangu Tana Bapa Mangu Loko* (Mother Guardian of the Earth Father Guardian of the Rivers) and *Inya Bokolo Bapa Bokolo* (Great Mother Great Father) are double gendered. Double gendered beings are common in Eastern Indonesia where ritual languages express notions of gender complementarity (Atkinson and Arrington 1990; McWilliam 2006).

While double-gendered characters exist, transgendered figures also exist in the form of spirit humans as well as human humans and nonhumans. A portrayal of Mother Seaworm in the name "Mother Seaworm Father Fish" points to the double-gendered or transgendered identity of this actor. The Seaworm Priests and other lower-ranking *Rato Marapu* (Marapu Priests and Elders) practice gender fluidity. *Rato Marapu* are biologically male and spend the majority of their time performing male roles, but periodically attach female symbols such as betel purses to themselves, and sometimes wear female garb such as women's shirts and purses (Photo 3.2). Elders who switch genders are transtaxa because they cross gender categories.

Some beings in the Kodi cosmos are trans-*field* because they switch their identities along modes of beings in addition to or instead of along the species and gender dimensions. Ra Hapu, the Lightning God, has the characteristics of an ancestor spirit as well as traits of a weather phenomenon. He is part spirit, part electrostatic surge. In its representation as Ra Hapu, lightning is the brightly lit bolt of electricity who embodies a deity. Lightning expresses the deity's power and his emotions. Lightning bolts are messages from Ra Hapu, and are thereby Ra Hapu's way of communicating (Fowler 2013; Hoskins 1998).

Taxa-crossing beings are key characters in the Kodi world-making cast. Clan and subclan ancestors, spirits, priests, lay persons, weather phenomena, marine creatures, and other figures cross taxa. In the biosocial relationships that make Kodi worlds, the beings who do the relating include double species, double gender, transspecies, transgender, and transfield creatures. Some beings reside on the Earth and others are celestial bodies. The collection of beings in the Sumba environment are actually linked in multispecies and transtaxa manifestations of "socio-natural enactments of world-making" (Tsing 2015, under "Abstract").[5] Seaworms are the main character of chapters 2 and 3 because they are magnificent tools, as Hoskins and other authors have shown, for finding the taxonomic links that bring items together into single taxonomic categories, such as items with "seaworm" in the names they are given by Kodi speakers and cognates for "seaworms" in Austronesian and Papuan languages. Seaworms also enable us to see links between seemingly disparate taxonomic categories, as they do here in this chapter for illuminating links between Mammalia and Polychaeta.

SEAWORMS IN ETHNOTAXONOMIES

In the Kodi worldview, people coexist with other living and nonliving entities in multispecies communities where transtaxa creatures live who are capable of

Photo 3.2   An Elder Carrying a Betel Purse and Wearing a Woman's Blouse While Harvesting Rice

transspecies communication (Kohn 2007). Describing a taxonomy populated by taxa-crossing beings in diverse communities provides a platform for exploring the contributions of ethnobiology to biosocial theory. A biosocial approach tracks the agency of more-than-human actants and sees ecological relationships as sites of sociocultural and biological production. If ethnobiology is the study of relationships among actants, a biosocial ethnobiology explores the ways actants construct taxonomic relationships. Ethnotaxonomy is the study of how classifications of actants influence the ways humans think about those actants and how they behave in relation to those actants. In a biosocial taxonomy, then, "ethno" is dropped as the prefix for "taxonomy" to recognize the power of more-than-human agency in the invention of the systems of classification that humans use. This raises the question of whether "ethno" needs to be dropped from "ethnobiology" so that we have a kind of "cannibal metaphysics" (Viveiros de Castro 2014) that dethrones humans from the pinnacle of taxonomic hierarchies. But, ethnobiologists prove through their excellent research and writing that, even with the "ethno" in "ethnobiology," ethnobiologists frame human-environment relationships in less-anthropocentric ways by drawing on the ways diverse social groups (i.e., the "ethno") cognize ecological relationships. The cognition of ecological relationships means the construction of human and nonhuman identities in the processes during which humans and nonhumans experience and interact with each other (Orr, Lansing, and Dove 2015). With this as a charge, then, we can explore questions such as the following: Do polychaetes have agency in determining their transtaxa status? Or is the ethnotaxonomic status of polychaetes driven by human identities and anthropocentric experiences (i.e., the cognition of polychaetes)?

NAMES FOR MARINE ORGANISMS

"Seaworms" appear in the ethnotaxonomies of Austronesian and Papuan people across Eastern Indonesia, Melanesia, and Polynesia. The great cultural value given to seaworms is a thread in communities across these regions, and is one of many clues that suggest historical relationships among communities and tie them together into one continuous culture area (Stewart and Strathern 2000). Polychaete biology is comparably spectacular throughout these regions where the brilliance of polychaetes creates similarly enchanting responses in human communities. "Seaworms" appears in comparable locations in the lexicons of not only Austronesian languages but also Papuan and mixed Austronesian-Papuan languages. In many communities throughout the Austronesian region, local words for "seaworms" identify marine species and other organisms, temporal periods in lunar calendars, ritual performances, and supernaturals.

Kirch and Green (2001) hold up *palolo* (PPN [Proto Polynesian] for "seaworms"[6]) as, "one of the most intriguing terms in PPN" (Kirch and Green 2001: 100). *Palolo* is an ancient term that was in the Proto Central Pacific (PCP) lexicon that preceded PPN, and that survives in contemporary Oceanic languages. Polychaetes are known as *palolo* or one of its cognates in Fiji (where the cognate is *balolo*), Futuna, 'Uvea, Tuvalu, Tokelau, the Cook Islands, the Society Islands, Tonga (the Tongan cognate is also *bu..olo*), Samoa, French Polynesia, Hawai'i, and perhaps additional locations. *Palolo* serves as linguistic evidence for reconstructions of ancient human migrations across Oceania, and supports the argument for "a PPN homeland in the Tonga-Samoa region" (Kirch and Green 2001: 100).

Nale is apparently not a cognate for the Eastern Polynesian term *palolo* or the Ambonese term *wawo*, although as a member of the Austronesian language family, numerous cognates for other words in Kodi exist as far away as Hawai'i, and may be due to the fact that both languages descend from Proto Austronesian. The terminology for "seaworms" is not geographically consistent in Eastern Indonesia; instead, a variety of terms exist. Nevertheless, evidence from the discursive and nondiscursive practices related to seaworms attests to the great time depth and the wide spatial extent of the human-polychaete relationship in Indo-Pacific worlds.

Numerous terms for seaworms are found throughout Eastern Indonesia where the Indigenous languages belong to either the Central-Eastern Malayo-Polynesian clade of Austronesian languages or to the Papuan family, and some languages contain a mixed Austronesian-Papuan lexicon due to contact. While evidence does not show that a single term and its cognates span this region, smaller clusters of languages contain cognates. Sumba's contemporary languages, for example, use similar terms. The Sumbanese languages are thought to have all descended from ancient Proto Sumba and, prior to that, from Proto Macro-Sumba, which descended from PCEMP and PAN (Blust 2008; Norquest and Downey 2013). The languages of contemporary Sumba include both Austronesian and Papuan elements that persist in Sumba's contemporary populations, and that aligns with the "genetic admixture between Austronesian farmers and indigenous Papuan populations" (Lansing et al. 2007: 16025).

Nale or *nyale* is the term for "seaworms" in the Kodi, Bukambero, Wejewa, Wanokaka, and Laboya languages of western Sumba. *Nyeli* or *ngeli* is the variant in Kambera, the language spoken by the majority of people in eastern Sumba (Forth, personal communication). *Nale* or *nyale* is also the term for seaworms among Sasak speakers on Lombok (Eklund 1977) and Tongo villagers in northwest Sumbawa (Welker 2009). Other terms found elsewhere in Eastern Indonesia are *wawo* and *laor* in Ambon; *oele* or *oelie* on Banda; *mechi* in the Austronesian Tetum language of East Timor (Palmer and de Carvalho 2008); and *mechi boot* in the Papuan Fataluku language spoken in East Timor (McWilliam 2006). Terms for "seaworms" from other locations beyond Eastern Indonesia are: *nút* in Vanuatu's Torres Islands and *un* in the Banks Islands; *vaien*, *lamaha*, and *kaama* in various places in Papua New Guinea; and *te nmatamata* and *te kawariki* in Kiribati (Schulze and Timm ...).

status of "seaworm" terms in Austronesian and Papuan ethnotaxonomies may vary. In the Kodi language,[7] the term *nale* references a generic-level taxon. The languages of some Sumbanese communities may contain species-level taxa for members of the *nale* class. For example, in the Laboya language, which is spoken by a community who are neighbors of the Kodi in western Sumba, *nyale* is the word for "seaworms" while *nare* refers to an inedible kind of seaworm that Laboya people say causes an itchy reaction if eaten (Geinaert-Martin 1992). In some Austronesian and Papuan communities, people recognize variations in the appearance and behavior of creatures within the "seaworm" taxa. Ambonese, for example, recognize differences in the size, color, and culinary qualities of the worms as well as in their swarming times (Pemungkas 2015). Color variations in worms occur among different species and also within different sexes of the same species. In *P. viridis*, female epitokes are blue-green while the male epitokes are orange-brown (Schulze and Timm 2012). Another instance of a possible polychaete species-level taxa is from Polynesia where eighteen contemporary languages in both western and eastern Polynesia have cognates of **weli*, the PPN name for a venomous sea worm (Kirch and Green 2001). **Ibo*, which is the Proto Oceanic word for an edible *Spinunculus* species (Blust and Trussel 2015), may also be a species-level taxa. In the Arosi language spoken in the Solomon Islands, *ogu* is a specific type of *palolo* seaworm (Blust and Trussel 2015). *Alitáptap* refers to a type of "glowworm, found on rocks at high tide" in the Aklanon language on the Philippine island of Panay (Blust and Trussel 2015). As more evidence becomes available, knowledge will increase about how Indigenous peoples conceptualize the taxonomic status of seaworms.

SEAWORMS IN LUNAR CALENDARS

Mondragon (2004: 289) writes, "local groups often create associations between the patterns and perturbations of the environment and cycles of human production which constitute organizing frameworks evocative of what western observers label 'calendars'" (Mondragon 2004: 289). Seaworms are one of the remarkable space-time patterns linking the traditional calendars of Eastern Indonesia, Melanesia, and Oceania. Seaworms appear in numerous space-time cultures as markers for annually repeating temporal intervals.

The synchrony of polychaete swarming with lunations, seasonal conditions, and other biotic phenomena, such as tree flowering and grain ripening, is resounded in the names for lunar months and the seasonal divisions in traditional calendars. These synchronies, patterns, and perturbations are the constituents of biosocial change.

Names that appear in both the Polynesian and the Eastern Indonesian annual calendars mark key points in seaworm reproductive biology, the Moon's phases, and the agricultural cycle. The names of some months refer to seaworms in numerous historical and contemporary examples in Eastern Indonesia and Oceania: in all of the Sumbanese languages, in Tetum, in native languages on Ambon, on Futuna, and elsewhere. In protohistoric Futuna, seaworms appear in the names of two months: *Palolo Mua* (Front/First Seaworms) when the first swarm appeared and *Palolo Muli* (Back/Last Seaworms) when the second swarm appeared (Kirch and Green 2001). In contemporary Kodi, one season and three months contain the local word for seaworms (see Table 2.1). The month names are *Wulla Nale Kiyo* (Little Seaworms Month), *Wulla Nale Bokolo* (Big Seaworms Month), and *Wulla Nale Wallu* (Return of the Seaworms or Last/Final Seaworms Month). The seaworm season begins in Little Seaworms Month and indicates the start of a new year and a new annual temporal cycle. The time of the seaworm festival in Futuna coordinates with the yam harvest, and in Kodi with the grain harvest. The contemporary Kodi and the ancient Futuna traditional calendars display similar patterns in the organization of time. The Futuna specify the final seaworm month as "back" or "last" and, likewise, the Kodi month names imply that the seaworms come "back" or "return," which is conceptually similar to the Futuna name. A difference is that the first Futuna month name uses "front" or "first" while the Kodi month name specifies "little" seaworms. Nevertheless, the marking by numerous cultures of nonhuman species' behaviors connect humans, animals, and plants into multispecies communities.

In some Polynesian languages, *palolo* identifies "a lunar month in the calendric system" (Kirch and Green 2001: 100), but Kirch and Green dismiss this appearance as unrelated to the seaworms. The marking in Polynesia is similar, however, to the Kambera case from eastern Sumba where people do not recognize seaworms in any rituals (Forth 1983), yet they have two months named after seaworms: *Ngeli Kudu* (Minor Seaworms Month) and *Ngeli Bokolo* (Major Seaworms Month) that respectively correspond to January–February and February–March in the Julian calendar. Thus, it might be possible that the loss of palolo in the ritual lives of people in Kambera and some parts of Polynesia occurred through historical change.

A cross-cultural, cross-regional tradition of naming units of time according to when the seaworms swarm existed at least as far back as when PCP was spoken by the "first Lapita settlers of the Fiji-Tonga-Samoa region"

(Kirch and Green 2001: 271), and may have even preexisted the evolution of PCP since parallel translations of the synchronous phenomena are found in bordering ethnolinguistic areas who also trace their heritage to Proto Central-Eastern Malayo-Polynesian and Proto-Austronesian. Descendants of Proto Austronesian speakers likely adjusted their calendar in response to variations in polychaete breeding seasons across the region.

SEAWORMS IN RITUAL PERFORMANCES

The convergences between seaworms, the Moon, and agropastoralism inspire ritual activities, and these associations have very long histories. The beginning of each new year is marked by first fruits celebrations, which typically involve an extended series of rituals. For the inland hamlets of contemporary western Sumba, the seaworm months correspond with the rice and millet harvests, which is when *Marapu* followers are obligated to perform *padolo* first fruits ceremonies. In contemporary Kodi, the three-month long seaworm season rites and the beginning of the year commence with *Wulla Nale Kiyo* (Little Seaworms Month). A comparable example from Oceania is Makahiki, the four-month long Hawaiian festival scheduled at the beginning of the new year and honoring Lono, the god of fertility, rain, and agriculture. In protohistoric Futuna, *fakaangiangi* was when the yams were harvested and the first fruits ritual feast was performed at the end of the month of *Palolo Muli* (Back/Last of the Seaworms). In Futuna, the rising of the polychaetes to the ocean surface is connected with the rising of Pleiades on the horizon at dusk (acronitic rising), the new Moon, and the yam harvest. Kirch and Green (2001) explain that these synchronies also determine the months that follow the *palolo* months:

> for the two lunations that must follow the **Palolo* months . . . *kelekele* may have been a month in which the yams, with earth adhering to them, are dug up. . . . The names of the next two lunations **Wai-mua* and **Wai-muli* are first and last rains . . . these months correspond with the end of the wet season in the Ancestral Polynesian area. . . . The wet season **taqu*—season of yam harvests and plenty—would have come to an end as Pleiades approached its acronitic setting around mid-March. The lunar names **Faka-qafu muli* and **Faka-qafu mate* presumably indicate the preparation of fields for yam planting at the transition from the wet season to the dry season. (Kirch and Green 2001: 272)

Another similarity that is found across Eastern Indonesia, Melanesia, and Oceania is the recognition of Pleiades's movement through the sky in calendrical names, and the association between Pleiades, the new year, and first fruits festivals. In the Kambera-speaking community on Sumba, *tula kawuru* (time of the Pleiades) corresponds with November–December. In the Native Hawaiian language, *Makali'i* corresponds with November–December, and is the temporal interval when Pleiades becomes visible just after sunset on the horizons of the Hawaiian islands. Some sources say that *Makali'i* is in October, a variation that Kirch and Green (2001) explain by the time when, 1000 years ago in ancient Hawai'i, the acronitic rising of Pleiades occurred; that is, in October–November. Another explanation may be that the naming of the months varied across the districts and islands of Hawai'i. *Makali'i* has at least twenty-four reflexes in Polynesia, attesting to its origins in Proto Oceanic. *Mataliki* is the PPN and Proto Oceanic term for Pleiades.

Kodi Rituals Involving Polychaetes

Calendrical time and spatial movement in Kodi culture are in sync with several elements of biosocial change. Depending on whether it is the seaworm season (*wulla nale*; also known as *kab'ba wei kapoke* [bland season]) or the bitter season (*wulla pad'du*), Kodi construct their worlds through either venturing out or staying home, by being "mobile with" (Jensen 2010) or being "still with," by getting rowdy or being quiet. Whereas the atmosphere in the bitter season is restrictive due to the many prohibitions on behavior, a free and festive atmosphere permeates the bland season. The hungry season is also known as the bitter season and includes *Wulla Paddu Laboya* (Laboya [the neighboring traditional domain in West Sumba] Bitter Month) followed by *Wulla Pad'du Kodi* (Kodi Bitter Month) and *Wulla Had'du* (Still/Silent Month). These are the months when celebratory feasts are taboo and people are encouraged to stay home, be still, fast, and not make loud noises by banging gongs, beating drums, or pounding grains. The bitter season is a dangerous time to travel because bodies cannot afford to lose scarce energy and because headhunters are actively seeking their prey. Kodi agropastoralists push back against famine by using creative strategies such as trading in open air markets, bartering with kin and allies (*mandara*), and gathering wild yams, ferns, grubs, and other famine foods. The seaworm season pulls people out of the hungry season when the grain baskets are depleted. The seaworm season is the time of the year when food becomes plentiful again, when farmers are able to restock their storage baskets and refatten their bodies. Rice and millet ripen in the fertile hill gardens and the polychaetes swarm in the warm ocean waters. The spatial and temporal rhythms of Kodi social life converge in the rituals that take place during the seaworm season. Seaworm season rituals occur along a space-time continuum that begins with divination ceremonies at polychaete swarming sites on the ocean reefs, followed by *haŋgapung* or *padolo* first fruits offerings, followed by the pilgrimage to the Great Clan Villages for the *pasola* jousting festival, and concluding with the return pilgrimage to coastal polychaete swarming sites. The seventh night after the full Moons of the Little Seaworms Month and the Kodi Bitter Season Month is, as a rule, the time for the opening rituals of the bland season and the bitter season, respectively.

The bland/seaworm season ritual complex is an extended sequence of divination rites, offerings, sacrifices, feasting, jousting, and pilgrimages. Many bland season rituals feature polychaetes. Seaworm Priests are the leaders of the bland season rituals and the heads of the entire annual ritual cycle. Currently, two Seaworm Priests hold religious positions in Kodi. The Seaworm Priests are the most powerful ritual authorities in Kodi's native *Marapu* religion. One of the Seaworm Priests lives in the Great Clan Village named Bukubani and the other lives in the Great Clan Village named Tossi. The two Seaworm Priests inherit their leadership positions along with the very "heavy" obligations to properly perform the many traditional rituals that occur throughout the annual cycle and to maintain the customary taboos attached to their positions. In 1998, the Seaworm Priest in Bukubani was Ghero Ndongo. He is the fifth generation Seaworm Priest who follows in the footsteps of his predecessors: his father Ra Ndenghe, his grandfather Wona Poka, his great-grandfather Rehe Ngoko, and his great- great-grandfather Winya Hangoko. The Seaworm Priests are similar to national presidents, according to Ghero Ndongo. Ghero Ndongo claims that, as the Seaworm Priest of Bukubani, he has control of the ritual calendar, of time, and of seaworms.

Seaworm Priests serve as the father figures for all Kodi people in Kodi Besar and its subsectors of Balla Hangale, Kodi Deta, and Kodi Wawa, as well as in Kodi Bandegdo and its subsectors of Balaghar and Bangedo. Seaworm Priests follow strict rules of conduct to ensure their constituents' security and wellbeing. These rules prescribe and proscribe their movements in correlation with the seasons. In the bland season, the Seaworm Priests move about their realms as they attend to their ritual duties, but during the bitter season the Seaworm Priests are *kabukut* (mourning), meaning they are bound to stay in their Great Clan Villages of Bukubani or Tossi. Great storms would cross over the island if they were they to leave their Villages. Riding their horses is taboo in the bitter season for them too because the riding would cause them to sway with their horses' gait, and the swaying would cause earthquakes. Looking at the world from the Kodi perspective, we find that the Seaworm Priests' actions have meteorological and geological consequences. In the Kodi worldview, the behavior of both clergy and lay people has good and/or bad consequences for diverse actants. A clear example comes from the idea that if one or more people act immorally, Mother Seaworm will not return for her annual visit, the polychaetes will not appear in the nearshore fisheries, the rains will be sparse, the drought will be long, the grain crops will fail, and famine will grip the community.

The seaworm ritual series that begins in the Little Seaworm Month with the Seaworm Priests' divination and consumption rites, continues in the Big Seaworm Month with *haŋgapung* rites. *Haŋgapung* are the first fruits offerings that Kodi farmers give to their immediate ancestors. *Haŋgapung* rites are performed in the graveyards in front of the minor *uma nale* (seaworm houses, or patrilineage houses) that are located in the garden hamlets (*kalimbiatu*). Women, the principal actors in *haŋgapung*, perform the rituals c̄ ̄e day before they travel to their Great Clan Villages for *pasola*. The w ̄men use wooden plates to bring rice, betel leaves, areca nuts, and money to the gravestones in the middle of their hamlets. The women call out to the *toyo mati* (dead people) as they throw the rice grains up into the air and toward the graves. They place the betel leaves, areca nuts, and money on the tops of the gravestones. Later in the day the women sacrifice chickens or, if they can afford them, dogs and pigs, which they offer to the ancestors during a shared meal. These are the gifts they offer to the dead people whose bodies are dead but whose souls are still present in the hamlets. The dead people will cry if the living descendants do not give them their share of the ritual commodities. When the dead people see the offerings, they know they need to be ready for the journey to the *pasola* fields.

The ancestors are due the "first fruits" of the rice harvest. If the first fruits are not given to the ancestors prior to living humans consuming the freshly harvested rice and prior to the pilgrimage to *pasola* and to *kadere nale* (gather seaworms), then the ancestors will punish their descendants for their neglect and disrespect. Across the Kodi territory, Kodi people grow a special, native variety of rice called *karanda* to use in the seaworm season rituals. *Karanda* is the variety that Biri Koni's body became when her parents sacrificed her in order to produce the first rice seeds, as recounted in the Biri Koni myth above. The rule that rice seeds must be from native varieties, not exotic or imported varieties, is an identity-claiming effort that links today's living agropastoralists to their ancestors who were the region's first farmers. Farmers throughout Kodi plant the native *karanda* variety together with an array of other native and non native varieties. *Karanda* is the fastest maturing variety. It is ready to harvest in the Big Seaworm Month or the Return of the Seaworms Month if farmers plant it as soon as the rainy season begins in the Kodi Bitter Month or the Nesting Month. When a household harvests their rice, they set aside a stash of *karanda* rice seeds in the *Mata Marapu* (Spirit Source), which are located in the ceiling rafters in the right front sections of subclan houses. The pseudonym for the sacred saved *karanda* seed is *ŋgaga nale* (seaworm rice), a name that acknowledges the religious and symbolic links between rice and polychaetes. The growers use the seaworm rice as offerings in the *haŋgapung* rites they perform in their hamlets prior to venturing off to the annual clan gatherings in Great Clan Villages where they participate in the *pasola* jousting festival. Soon thereafter, householders carry some of the seaworm rice with them to use as offerings in the rites they perform in the Great Clan Villages during *pasola*. Farmers also save *karanda* seeds for replanting in their gardens in the next year's Bitter Kodi Month and Nesting Month. They store the seeds in their houses from harvest time until the seaworm season rites of *haŋgapung* and *pasola*, and the subsequent growing season.

ʻe ritual space-time rhythm is *haŋgapung* in the uplands for the pa. aeage subclan's ancestors, *pasola* on the coast for the whole clan's ancestors. After *haŋgapung* is complete and the lineage ancestors have given their permission, the hamlet-dwellers are free to make the pilgrimage to the Great Clan Villages for *pasola*. *Pasola* is performed near the seaworm gathering sites and next to the major *Uma Nale* (Seaworm Clan Houses), also known as the *Uma Marapu Moro* (Medicine Spirit Houses) in the coastal *Parona Bokolo* (Great Clan Villages). While the Kodi householders direct *haŋgapung* rituals in their rural hamlets, the two Seaworm Priests are in charge of the rituals in the Great Clan Villages at Bukubani and Tossi. As in *haŋgapung*, *pasola* performers honor the ancestors with chanted prayers and material offerings. As they say their prayers, *pasola*-goers place bits of rice, betel leaves, and areca nuts, on the tops of their ancestors' graves.

Like the first fruit offerings of rice, the ancestors receive the first portions of the seaworms in the form of offerings made in people's homes in their garden hamlets, and also in the patriclan homes in the Great Clan Villages. The locations of the first fruit rituals that accompany the seaworm harvest occur in reverse order from the *haŋgapung* offerings of the first fruits of rice. With rice, the first fruits offerings are in the hamlets and then on the coast in the Great Clan Villages. For seaworms, people first perform rituals on the coast in seaworm swarming sites and subsequently in their upland hamlets.

The pilgrimages to deliver the first fruits from the rice and seaworm harvests are particular kinds of co-mobility between people and other species that take place along particular routes through the landscape and seascape. The mobilizations affect humans in a variety of ways through changes in activity levels, nutrition, spirituality, and sociality. Pilgrims travel from all parts of Kodi to gather polychaetes, from nearby hamlets in the coastal plains to faraway hamlets in the upland corners of the region. The ritual seaworm harvest occurs only in specially designated swarming sites. The location for the rituals has changed over time. Halete Beach was the site on March 20, 1998 (Photo 3.3). In the past, the location was *Wee Dangga*, which is the name of the most sacred site in the region and was a settlement located in the domain of Bukambero, which is in the northeast sector of Kodi. The seaworm origins myth recounted above identifies *Limmo Manu* as the sacred site where seaworms swarmed long ago.

Photo 3.3   Halete Beach, the Location for the Ritual Seaworm Gathering on March 20, 1998

The location of seaworm swarms is a topic that has entered into the ethnohistories of western Sumbanese communities. The Seaworm Priest of Bukubani, Ghero Ndongo, claims that his predecessors gave seaworms to the neighboring domains of Wanokaka and Laboya who did not have seaworms in the past and who could not access seaworms without the Kodi Seaworm Priests' permission. This claim by the Rato Nale of Bukubani is a political maneuver related to identity, power, and territory. The Kodi tactic is similar to the one Palmer and de Carvalho (2008) describe from the Tutuala subdistrict of East Timor where community leaders invite a wider audience to their seaworm harvesting rituals in order to publicly display their right to control the local political economy. Hoskins (1993) describes similar claims by other ritual elders in Kodi, and explains the competing claims as political contestations. The Laboya people concur that Kodi is the source of their seaworms, and they point to the fact that more seaworms spawn on beaches in Kodi than in Laboya (Geinaert-Martin 1992). Geinaert-Martin writes,

> According to some modern-minded Sumbanese, including some Laboya people, [the] relative lack of *nyale* may be due to the fact that currents and waves are particularly violent in the bay of Laboya. According to more traditional Laboya elders, the absence of the *nyale* dates back to the time when a *rato* [priest/elder] of Hodana [a village] failed to obey the many taboos that prevailed at the time of

Padu [Bitter Season]. Whatever the value of these explanations may be, for the Laboya, although the *nyale* remain invisible for the most part, they are believed to arrive on the beach in great quantities and their coming is expected with great joy, just as in Kodi and in Wanokaka. (Geinaert-Martin 1992: 287)

Ghero Ndongo's statement and the information Geinaert-Martin collected give voice to ideas about the relationships between these four western Sumbanese ethnolinguistic communities of Kodi, Laboya, Wanokaka, and Guara. The relationship is described in ethnohistories and manifested in the historical direction of the flow of the seaworm exchange. Ghero Ndongo's claim, which is verified by Geinaert-Martin's interlocutors, is to historical precedence in the ownership of a vital resource that is one among numerous bases for authority and power. These social dynamics illustrate the liveliness of identity politics, and its connections to polychaetes and territory as critical resources.

Singing in the Seaworms

On their trips to the beaches, the Kodi people who pilgrimage to gather seaworms travel to swarming sites during the day (Photo 3.4), usually arriving in time to swim, play, sing, and socialize from the daylight into the nighttime hours. The pilgrims wade through the shallows holding burning torches and flashlights, and the seaworms flock to their lights. The pilgrims scoop up their harvest using their special *kaleku bokot* (harvest purses) and *kaleku nale* (seaworm baskets). Throughout the night, the pilgrims sing to each other and to Mother Seaworm, summoning her back into their hands and mouths. Kodi pilgrims nowadays gather seaworms throughout the night, similar to the Ambonese gatherers 335+ years ago when seaworms were "caught from 6 pm until the Moon rises . . . [and] the population celebrates with music and dance" (Horst 1902, under "Under the Wawo").

Nowadays in Kodi celebrants sing, "*Magho Inya Nale* (Come Mother Seaworm)! *Magho Bapa Ipu Mbaha* (Come Father Fish)." Their lyrical pleas reveal the goddess to be a spirit with a double-gendered or transgendered identity. The singers describe Mother Seaworm Father Fish as both an eligible bachelorette and a handsome stallion. She is a polychaete as well as an equine who also has human-like traits. She is human human and spirit human. She is transtaxa.

The goddess would not know she was welcome and therefore would not return every year if the land-dwellers did not express their desire to commune with her. Sometimes, even though they tell her how much they desire her presence, she does not return or, as in the case of the 1997 seaworm swarming event, only a few instances of her returns. Her non-return indicates her displeasure with the morality, or lack of it, among her people.

Photo 3.4   Pilgrimage to Halete Beach for the Ritualized Seaworm Gathering

"When we summon Mother Seaworm and she doesn't come to us," according to a seaworm gatherer, "it is because too many Kodi people have sinned. But, if she comes, she will stay here and provide for us all the way until the next Rainy Season [i.e., the following *Wulla Pad'du Kodi* or *Wulla Hab'bu*]."

The gatherer who is quoted above portrays Mother Seaworm as a maternal figure who promotes good behavior and punishes bad behavior. She is a provider and nourisher who is willing to sacrifice her own body for the sake of her followers. For others, specifically for the Seaworm Priests, Mother Seaworm is less like a mother and more like a lover. She is a beautiful woman who returns for yearly private rendezvous with her men if they properly woo her and if, still, the Priests' followers—men and women—have behaved themselves in the preceding months. The differing relationships that Mother Seaworm has with the Priests on the one hand and with the general populous on the other hand illuminate the hierarchy in the *Marapu* religion where the Priests have higher status than the parishioners. Relationships between Mother Seaworm, the Priests, and the general populous reproduce the social hierarchy in Kodi.

People court not only the seaworm companions but also human mates during the seaworm season. The performance of the "Come Mother Seaworm, Come Father Fish" chant represents the genre of courting songs/rites known

as *kawoking*. In the Big Seaworm Month, when the rice harvests are under-
way, young people go *kawoking*, meaning they hang out at the beach together
where they sing, talk, play, and search for their true sweethearts. Kodi, in
their emic perspectives on the history of their world, connect the rituals of
the seaworm season with the reproduction of society. The seaworm festivities
thus link marriage and procreation in the mythical past with marriage and
reproduction in the current times.

Just prior to dawn, the pilgrims return home with their bounty (Photo 3.5).
Once the pilgrims return to their hamlets with the newly harvested seaworms,
they fetch their special *kandoro nale* (bamboo seaworm tubes) and empty
out the ripe relish they stuffed in the tubes during the previous year's ceremonies. The pilgrims eat this together with their families in a shared meal. These
ritual victuals deliver a powerful nutritional boost for the hungry pilgrims
and their families at the end of the hungry season. The female *Palolo* sp. epitokes in the *wawo* swarms from which Ambonese gather are 54.72 percent
protein, 12.12 percent carbohydrate, 11.67 percent fat, and 10.78 percent ash
(Pemungkas 2015). The seaworm meals are valuable in the health of the children, women, and men who have been subsisting on meager diets in good years
and on famine foods in bad years, and who are simultaneously facing energy
output demands at the beginning and into the height of the grain harvest season.

The seaworm harvest from the current year is stuffed into *kandoro nale* and
left to sit for four nights. After four nights, the pilgrims extract the seaworms
and mix them together with *ndaga nale* literally meaning "the seaworm
guard" (Labiatae[8]), chili peppers (*Capsicum* Solanaceae), and salt. The relish
makers stuff the newly prepared seaworm relish into the *kandoro nale*. The
householders stash the *kandoro nale* next to the *kaleku weiha* (sacred rice
baskets) and *kalidi wini* (sacred winnowing trays), *tobbo wini* (sacred seed
gourd), and *kobbo wini* (sacred coconut bowls) in the *Mata Marapu* (Spirit
Sources) of their houses, where they also put the *ŋgagha nale* (seaworm rice).
The special seaworm relish remains there until the following year when the
householders collect new batches of seaworms.

Collectively, Kodi people must eat their quota of seaworms every Return of
the Seaworms Month or else risk many negative consequences throughout the
subsequent annual cycle. Rehi Winye, a grandmother who no longer makes
the pilgrimage to the swarming sites herself, but instead relies on her children
to go and bring home some seaworms to share with her said, "We have to eat
at least a little bit of seaworms every year. If I do not eat any seaworms at all,
I will not be well."

Rehi Winye cooks the seaworms in coconut milk to which she adds *ndaga
nale*, chilis, and salt. Consuming even small portions of the polychaete deli-
cacies ensures her wellbeing. People's acts of consumption are multispecies
interactions that demonstrate the incorporation of invertebrates by vertebrates,

Photo 3.5   A Man and Child Carrying Seaworms on the Return Pilgrimage Home from the Seaworm Ritual

and the intersubstantiality of beings. My focus in this chapter has been on a particular group of ocean creatures. Through an ethnobiologically-informed biococial approach, I have shown that the reproductive biology of polychaetes is a key part of the foundation for human wellbeing.

CONTROLLING CULTURAL IDENTITY AND PROTECTING BIOSOCIAL INTEGRITY

By engaging with the seaworms, Kodi people ensure their society's integrity. To maintain social integrity in this case means to authenticate the community's privileged identity. The seaworms may appear in other Sumbanese domains, but their origins are in Kodi. The society's historical foundation and its claim to territorial rights are evidenced in the three months in the ritual calendar with seaworms in their names. Seaworms index the cycles of time, the lunar year, and the historical depth of this community in this place. Kodi people identify with seaworms because the first seaworms were the body of a Kodi woman; not a not a Wanokaka or Laboya or Kambera woman. The titles of *Marapu*'s highest religious officials, the Seaworm Priests, attest to the claim Kodi have over the seaworms. The Seaworm Priests entice Mother Seaworm with their invitations to romantic rendez-vous. As if that were not enough to lure the mother goddess, swarms of Kodi people gather on the beach to sing love songs to her. The mother goddess would not return were it not for their deep desires for her. Proper relations with the seaworms' various apparitions are as essential to wellbeing as the availability of marine resources and garden crops are. Mother Seaworm enables the reproduction of a multispecies and transtaxa world. If she does not come forth, neither do the seaworms nor the grain crops, nor the Rice Goddess Biri Koni, nor the people's health because these beings belong to "a socio-spiritual continuum" (Viveiros de Castro 2014: 53). Human sensations, experiences, and cognition within this kind of world is the substance of their identity.

A phenomenological understanding of Kodi cosmology may propose that "cognition lies between subjective experience and social identity" (Orr, Lansing, and Dove 2015: 160). This phenomenological understanding is based on studying nondiscursive practices and embodiment (Orr, Lansing, and Dove 2015). Understanding the ways people cognize space-time depends also on describing language, symbols, and actions as these are among the means through which people express their sensations and perceptions. Combining the phenomenological and biosocial approaches with cognitive and interactive ones makes room for including meaning and feeling in attempts to understand the cognition of biosocial change.

The activities of people in relation to seaworms explain certain space-time aspects of society and nature in Kodi. "Start[ing] with the sea worms" (Hoskins 1993: 80) pointed Hoskins toward a study of time, and pointed me toward the study of time *and* space. In the broader biosocial context, polychaetes signify spatiotemporal change. In Kodi's multispecies biosociety, humans and polychaetes change while interacting with other beings.

CHANGE AS RESPONSE AND CORRESPONDENCE IN MULTISPECIES COMMUNITIES

Change is response and correspondence. In the people-spirit-plant-animal network, transformations are responses to co-inhabitants' activities. The space-time culture of people is partly composed of responses to the activities of nonhumans (as we will see in the next chapter to be true in relation to seaworms and the Moon). Likewise, the reproductive biology of polychaetes is partly a response to lunar periodicity. Cyclical changes in the Moon are responses to various forces in the Multiverse (again, more on this in the next chapter). Assessing the episodic encounters that occur between the polychaetes and people illuminates how numerous actants change together. Analyzing people's conceptualizations of space-time and attempting to understand the agency of polychaetes provides entré into the ways multispecies communities change.

The ongoing changes that are occurring in society and in ecology are co-constructed in multispecies, transtaxa interactions. As they work together and come to correspond to one another, seaworms, people, and the many other actants who participate in the seaworm season transform their biosocial realities. Many types of beings continuously engage with one another in the exchanges and encounters that form and maintain the biosocial networks that constitute Kodi society. Members of the transspecies, transgender, transfield Kodi collective interact through exchanges of material substances and immaterial phenomena. Now is the right time to comment on the term "interactions" that I have thus far been using in this book in reference to what humans and polychaetes do in relation to one another and the alternative term "correspondences" (Ingold 2013: 15). When he uses "correspondences," Ingold is working to redefine the theory of evolution and the idea that species are separate and distinct from one another rather than mutually constituted. Ingold causes us to think of the lives of organisms as continuously unfolding in relation to one another over the course of the lifespan of individuals and over multiple generations. As organisms swap material and nonmaterial components of themselves, they make others. As they encounter material and nonmaterial components of others, they make themselves.

Polychaetes index the state of the environment as well as changing eco-logical conditions by delivering information to other individuals in their own taxa and to beings who belong to other taxa. The polychaetes provide information to other species through their composition, function, and behav-ior. Polychaetes are sources of information about the "evolution of complex invertebrates . . . invertebrate reproduction and development" (Glasby and Fauchald 2007, under "What are Polychaetes?"). Polychaetes' colors, shapes, and behaviors (e.g., the release of possibly toxic bioluminescent substance in some species) inform potential predators whether or not they are game, and potential prey whether or not they are threats. As bioindicators, seaworms inform scientists about the health of marine ecosystems (Glasby and Fauchald 2007) through their responses to the changing conditions of their habitat. Through their swarming behaviors, seaworms deliver information to Kodi people about the Moon's phases, the spirits' emotions and activities, future crop yields, the integrity of society, and ecosystems health. When harvesting from the spawning swarms, people rearrange polychaete eggs and sperm, siphon out the worms' fertile segments, and possibly affect the percentage of successful fertilizations and/or halt the development of the trocophore larvae.

Some communities in the Indo-Pacific region promote the ritualized gath-ering and consumption of seaworms as examples of sustainable traditional resource management (Palmer and de Carvalho 2008). But the sustainability of harvesting practices is uncertain, and probably varies depending on the location and species in question. Mining officials, in an attempt to deflect blame for their own environmentally destructive practices, accuse Sumbawan villagers of overharvesting seaworms nearly to the point of extinction, and damaging coral reefs through the use of destructive techniques for harvesting fish, octopus, shellfish, and seaweed (Welker 2009). One species whose con-servation status is suspected of being depleted by human predation is *Palolo viridis*, which occurs in Indonesia's Lesser Sunda Islands, Samoa, American Samoa, Rarotonga, Kiribati, Fiji, the Solomon Islands, Vanuatu, Papua New Guinea, and elsewhere. The IUCN Redlist shows palolo as a Threatened spe-cies, but qualified this designation with a statement about insufficient data that prevents certainty about its status. The tentative listing is based upon evidence from Samoilys and Carlos (1990) who found that overconsump-tion may have caused local extinction of the species on Samoa's Upolu Island (World Conservation Monitoring Centre 1996). On the other hand, some communities' traditional ecological management systems do include mechanisms to regulate harvests that would hypothetically prevent the deple-tion of species. The traditional resource management system in Kodi, for example, contains conservation mechanisms. The traditional resource man-agement system proscribes polychaete harvests from only one or two specific beaches on only one or two specific days of the lunar year, with prohibitions preventing the harvest of polychaetes from those beaches on any other days. The harvest taboos are backed by the belief that people who gather poly- chaetes at nonsanctioned times will be bitten by the *baŋga marapu* (spirit dogs) who guard the polychaete spawning sites. Spirit dogs are the source of the name *pa ice baŋga* (dogs see it) given to the first phase of the Moon because these dogs have the special ability to see the miniscule new Moon in its reincarnation after its "death" during the dark of the Moon. Clearly, spirit dogs are completely entangled with the multispecies conceptualization of the world through their relationships with the Moon, people, and polychaetes. Whether or not sustainable harvesting is an actual or potential effect of the belief in spirit dogs is unknown.

In this era of great concern about overall biodiversity and the health of our oceans, we need to know how humans interact with marine life. Ethnobiology is an important science for simply inventorying biodiversity in particular loca- tions, and also for building knowledge about the behavior of living beings. Through documenting relationships between humans and nonhumans, ethno- biologists deepen and expand knowledge about habitats, ecosystems health, and the world-making activities of both humans and nonhumans. This is true for terrestrial, marine, atmospheric, and extraterrestrial environments. We need to understand the human dimensions of Earth's seascapes and land- scapes in order to know how human sensations, perceptions, cosmologies, knowledges, actions, and behaviors affect nonhuman populations. People's ideas and practices have implications for the viability and resiliency of our co-inhabitants of this Multiverse.

In addition to being biological indicators, polychaetes are ecosystem engi- neers who modify their marine habitats. Polychaetes are nutrient recyclers who process food and waste in aquaculture systems. They are reef engineers who build reefs by living in tubes and affect reefs by boring holes (Glasby and Fauchald 2007). They attract predators to feed at certain times in particular places when they swim to and wriggle around on the surface to breed. Poly- chaetes subsist mainly on algae and are near the base of food chains so their behaviors, population levels, and other characteristics have material effects on their predators, including the fish, shellfish, birds, and humans who eat them. The preys' physical substance constitutes the physical substance of the predators, and the predators' actions affect the character of the prey's popu- lation. Human behaviors affect polychaetes' space-time traits via the ways humans interact with polychaetes when they are breeding. Here is evidence for the mutual constitution of beings in multispecies communities. These are reciprocal relationships with very deep timelines and very extensive spatial distribution, since polychaetes have populated Earth's oceans for at least 540 million years dating back to the Middle Cambrian (Glasby and Fauchald 2007). The entanglements are so long term and significant, that we might speculate that, in the words of a social theorist, "reciprocal interpretations of behavioral and environmental signs" (Descola 2014: 272) between swarming polychaetes and gathering humans has involved human-polychaete coevolution, or "reciprocal evolutionary change," in the words of an evolutionary biologist (Thompson 2005: 3).

As prey who live near the bottom of the food chain, polychaetes' behaviors influence the presence and abundance of humans and other predators. Polychaetes are like the "shrimps [who] would not be eaten by baleen whales unless they made large homogenous swarms of heavy concentrations or patches" (Russell and Yonge 1974: 267). Kodi people swarm to feed because polychaetes swarm. The agency of polychaetes in the space-time practices of humans is significant. This is evident in festive gatherings of humans in the same spaces and at the same times as swarms of polychaetes are there. These swarming collectives of humans and nonhumans are multispecies aggregates. Polychaete behaviors cause other species to move along certain routes at specific times, and thus coproduce the space-time dimensions of those species. Kodi people recognize the synchronized patterns in the reproductive biologies of living beings, lunar periodicity, and seasonality. The space-time dimensions of polychaetes are their emplacements and their movements at specific times and the information they deliver in the course of moving through space-time.

Studying human-polychaete correspondences leads to explanations of the human cognition of biosocial patterns and processes. Here in this chapter, I discussed temporality, like Hoskins and other Sumbanese and Eastern Indonesian ethnographers do (e.g., Forth 1982; Fox 1979). Similar to these ethnographers, I also am concerned with the anthropological issues of meaning, agency, communication, and expression. My broader goal has been to use temporality and spatiality to gain insights into the cognition of biosocial change. What do people know about biosocial change? How does knowledge about change link to the ways people perceive and relate to their surroundings? This concern is determined by both my upbringing in the subfield of ecological anthropology and heightened attention to global change across the sciences as well as in lay culture.

When Kodi people translate biosocial patterns and processes into their own cultural context the Moon, like the polychaetes, denotes space-time. Actually, "the Moon is the most important unit in Kodi time reckoning" (Hoskins 1993: 69). Yet, likewise, we should not think that polychaete rhythms, Moon phases, and seasonal patterns fully determine how Kodi people organize space-time. This is a multispecies community, after all, with myriad influential members. Kodi people recognize the cosmos as being a multispecies community when we define that concept as a collection of human and nonhuman beings; of body-bound living beings and of freely moving spiritual beings; of beings before, during, and after life; and of living and nonliving entities. Their cosmology may provide a biosocial platform from where we might gain insights into what it means to live in multispecies worlds from perspectives other than the human one. Experiencing the environment from the polychaetes', the Moon's, or any nonhuman's position is challenging if not impossible given our human limitations, but the Kodi culture provides its individual humans with the justifications as well as the techniques for attempting to understand these nonhumans' experiences.

By elaborating on the biosocial relationships between people and ̄ y- chaetes, a pivotal relationship in the Sumbanese sea/land-scape, we sc ̄ ̄that the beings who live in multispecies communities are mutually constituted. In multispecies communities, the composition, structure, and function of the constituent entities are shaped in relationships with one another and are moderated by external and internal factors, as has been described above. In the actual world of biosocial relations, polychaetes and humans interact not alone but together with many other entities. The marine benthic worms like the humans who co-reside in Kodi's biosociety are ecosystem engineers (Wright and Jones 2006) who modify one another's habitats, biologies, and social activities.

For many generations, the Austronesian and Papuan peoples who have inhabited the Indo-Pacific islands have been doing the difficult intellectual work of translating their experiences with and careful observations of their island communities into their space-time cultures. This is the work of constructing biosocial knowledge and making biosocial worlds. They do this work not alone as humans but as members of a collective of beings. The polychaetes feed humans—literally with the substance of their bodies and intellectually with the periodicity of their breeding and their other biosocial traits. Whereas the polychaetes are actants, the Moon and planets are also. The light that the Sun and Moon send to the Earth's surface signals to the polychaetes when they ought to breed. The Moon's rhythms tell people when to collect polychaetes, as well as when to schedule their bland season and bitter season rituals. Other names in the Kodi calendar contain information about monsoonal rhythms that people use to construct space-time: calendrical flowering of the *mboka* and *katoto* trees and the regular emergence of the *mangata* mushrooms. In Futuna, the months other than the *Palolo* months take space-time signals from yams, Pleiades, sea turtles, and turmeric (Kirch and Green 2001). The actants differ in differently-located communities because of differences in seasonality, flora, fauna, and other ecological characteristics, which points to another point of nonhuman agency: "critical changes in ritual architecture with major implications for Pacific [and Indo-Pacific] archaeology" (Kirch and Green 2001: 274) followed the ancient Austronesians as they moved southward into Eastern Indonesia and eastward into Melanesia and the Pacific. In other words, human traces in and effects on sea/landscapes drove and were driven by changes in the human organization of time that were driven by and also drove spatial changes. Biosocial variations are time-space transformations.

NOTES

The Biri Koni myth has many different versions. (Hoskins [1993] records at le.   ur stories about the origins of seaworms, and discusses the reasons why more than one version of the story exists.) The version of the Biri Koni myth that I present is a synthesis of the overlapping ideas in the different versions plus some important points made by religious authorities. Several other ethno-theories about the origins of crops are held by people who are Catholics and Protestants. These stories reflect the teachings of the Christian church. I do not consider these stories in the present analysis. A comparison between the various theories about crop origins might be the subject of future analyses.

2. In this context "food" refers to garden crops, specifically rice. Throughout Sumba and Indonesia rice is often synonymous with food. In Kodi the generic term for food (*ŋagha*) is also one of the several terms for rice.

3. The opening to this myth is a story about the way the storyteller views Kodi identity. The storyteller refers to hunter gatherer communities on Sumba which may reflect a belief that hunter gatherer communities occupied the island simultaneously with horticulturalists. Placing the hunter gatherers on Earth and the horticulturalists "Above" signifies a hierarchical relationship where hunter gatherers have lower status relative to horticulturalists. The storyteller also expresses the idea that the horticulturalists initially refused to trade with the hunter gatherers. Eventually, though, the segregated island populations integrated. If one were to connect the myth (which admittedly are stories people tell themselves about themselves and not historically-accurate records) we might see the history archaeologists and historians tell about the settlement of islands in this region by, first, Papuan hunter gatherers and, later, Austronesian horticulturalists, the early contact between groups, and their subsequent integration. This historical model is actually reflected now in the Kodi language and genetics which are mixtures of Papuan and Austronesian.

4. One narrator of this myth made a distinction between the rice cultivars that sprouted from Biri Koni's body and rice cultivars that were introductions "from the government." "The government" is a term which refers to any non-Indigenous organization not just administrators from the Indonesian national or regional agencies.

5. This quote from Tsing is actually her definition of "landscapes." I use her words here to define "multispecies and transtaxa" because multispecies and transtaxa communities are part of landscapes. Using this definition and taking landscapes to be like multispecies communities, transtaxa communities aligns with anthropological theories of culture as "world-making."

6. "Palolo" is a widespread term in the Polynesian Pacific. "Palola" is the scientific name, inspired by the Polynesian name, of the genus to which the palolo species

belongs. The *Palola* genus contains at least 14 species grouped into two clades and several subclades (Schulze 2006; Schulze and Timm 2012).

7. Kodi is one of eight Sumba languages in the Sumba Hawu subgroup of the Central-Eastern Malayo-Polynesian group of the Malayo-Polynesian branch of Austronesian.

8. In 1998, I collected a botanical voucher of *ndaga nale* and deposited it in the Bogor Herbarium. Scientists at the Bogor Herbarium identified that vouchers as *Ocimum sanctum* L. Lamiaceae. Based on his own survey, Dammerman (1926) identified *ndaga nale* as *Hyptis suaveolens* (L.) Poit Lamiaceae. Verheijen (1984) also observed *ndaga nale* on Sumba and identified it as *Ocimum basilicum* L. Lamiaceae. Lamiaceae is the family for all three of these identifications.

Chapter 4

Connecting with Celestial Bodies and Un-Grounding Space-Time

THE BIOSOCIAL STRINGS ATTACHED

Are abiotic entities social beings? We might be able to discern abiotic species who are social in ways similar to how we distinguish between social and non-social species within the biotic world. Social biotic species—such as microbes, ants, bees, dogs—receive attention because their sociality is inherently fascinating, and also because it implicates them as engineers of human bodies and ecosystems (e.g., Benezrá, DeStefano, and Gordon 2012; Herdobler and Wilson 1990; Heyes and Galaef 1996; Kohn 2007). Abiotic entities might also be cast as social beings if we consider their relationships with one another and their influences within human societies. I argue here that human societies are more-than-human; they are universal biosocial collectives.

The universal biosocial collectives that human societies belong to include abiotic entities in the same sense that they include nonhuman biotic species. Some abiotic entities have greater influence than others on human sociality depending on which entities exist within a society's landscapes and which entities are present in the ideas and practices of the human collective. Cross-culturally, particular abiotic entities are more or less present in the social lives of people. The ways abiotic entities implicate themselves in human societies hinges upon those entities' own biophysical characteristics as well as the ways humans deal with them socioculturally.

The abiotic entities that play both biophysical and sociocultural roles in human worlds exist not only on Earth but also beyond Earth. Two of the "Outer Space" entities who play especially big social roles across cultures are the Moon and Sun. While the Moon and Sun are merely two objects within a vast universe of objects that interact with Earth and everything/everybody on

Earth, they are the two objects that I will use here to encourage theorists to extend their idea of the "social" to abiotic entities.

The Moon and the Sun are "social" abiotics. The Moon and Sun have strongly influential relationships with the Earth with whom they form a vast yet, at the same time, tiny network: vast because of the amount of space-time involved, and tiny within the context of the whole universe. On the macroscopic level, the gravitational energy of the universe's massive objects warps space-time, sculpts objects' shapes, sets objects' orbital paths, and binds together the objects in our universe. Examples of massive objects are the Earth, Moon, and Sun, which define space-time as they relate to one another and to the universe's other coexistents. The Earth, Moon, and Sun gravitate toward one another, causing the Moon to rotate around the Earth, and the Earth-Moon to rotate around the Sun as a unit.

The Earth, Moon, and Sun engage in relationships with each other and with other celestial bodies that define space-time. These astronomical objects exert gravitational forces that shape other objects' bodies and orbits. The Sun sends its heat and light energy 93 million miles to Earth making it inhabitable for all of this planet's species. The Moon's radiation delivers light to Earth from 230,100 miles away. The temporality of the Earth and Moon's rotational orbits structure the days, months, years, seasons, and tides. The objects affect one another too by causing changes (in addition to regularities) through time in fluctuating ocean and air currents, climate, weather, rotation speeds, and geological processes. These are merely some of the geophysical factors that shape the biosocial contexts within which Earth's biotics emerge in relation to the universe's biotics and abiotics. The forms and functions of Earth and its living and nonliving components continuously emerge as the Earth, Moon, and Sun engage with one another and with the other objects, forces, and processes in our universe.

The social collective to which we humans, nonhuman species, the Earth, the Moon, and the Sun all belong is identifiable by different labels depending on the scale. We might call it the 9-trillion-mile long solar system, or the 100,000-light-years-long Milky Way Galaxy, or the more than 46 billion light-year-big universe. Compared to the universe, which is 13.8 billion years old, the Earth is a comparatively young 4.543 billion years old, and the Moon is only slightly younger at 4.53 billion years old. Every known existent—living and nonliving—belongs to the universe. All space, time, matter, and energy are members of the ginormous universe, and interact with one another in some form or the other. Physicists and other space-oriented scientists describe the "nature" of the universe. Here in chapter 4 I demonstrate that the universe is "social" as well in the sense that biosocial relationships bind together its constituents. Earthbound human's relationships with non-Earthbound living and nonliving existents define all of the universe's constituents as biosocial beings. This is the point I elaborate upon here in this chapter with details about the relations between the universe's constituents as represented in Kodi cosmology.

THE CELESTIAL PERSPECTIVE

Anthropologists have long pursued the goal of describing and explaining the multiple perspectives that communities of humans have on the world. Within the single *Homo sapiens* species anthropologists have documented ⌐ at cognitive, perceptual, and sensual diversity that might—in collaboratio ⹁ith political, economic, emotional, physiological and other forms of diversity— lead to the construction and continuous emergence of a community's cosmology; that is, a collectively-shared perspective on what we science-influenced Westerners refer to as the "universe." Contemporary social theorists who are working in the veins of multispecies ethnography (e.g., Hartigan 2015) and posthuman studies (Viveiros de Castro 2014) advocate for adopting the perspectives of nonhuman living species. Are anthropologists also capable of adopting the perspectives of the nonliving? Can ethnographic strategies (Whitehead 2009), such as the emic/etic frame, enable social theorists to capture the perspectives of nonhuman, nonliving, "natural" objects?

Here in chapter 4, I experiment with seeing the world through the Moon's and Sun's eyes by presenting the ways Kodi people perceive the Moon's and Sun's perceptions and actions combined with information about these objects from scientific astronomy's perspectives. In Kodi cosmology, what does the world look like from the Moon's point of view? From the Kodi perspective, what does the world look like from the Sun's point of view?

Studying Kodi cosmology enables us to see the *sky* from the *field* and the *field* from the *sky*. Kodi people see astronomical bodies from personal/ cultural/human perspectives and they also give those entities their own personal/cultural/transbeing perspectives. In certain settings, Kodi people describe space objects' perspective by taking a human perspective on nonhuman perspectives. Kodi people also, in certain ritual settings, negotiate their relationships with astronomical beings. Kodi people's understandings of their astronomical companions come from sensing, observing, and experiencing, as well as from knowledge they have learned from multiple sources, including their families, friends, and through institutions such as schools, churches, governments, and media sources. Kodi translate all of the information that is available to them about the space beyond Earth into a cosmology where they subjectify visible astronomical objects.

The model of a biosocial universe is ethnographically grounded in Kodi cosmology, as illustrated in the passages below. Contemporary social theory lends structure to the idea of the universe as a society. Contemporary social theory also inspires thinking about the universe's inhabitants as biosocial beings (e.g., Ingold 2013; Palsson 2013). Scholars push us to consider "human relations with nonhumans" (Kohn 2013: 7) and to "repopulate the social sciences with nonhuman beings" (Descola 2014: 268).

Yet, scholars most commonly include only "species" or "organisms"— i.e., living nonhumans—in their pleas to extend anthropology's purview. Some exceptions are Descola (2013: 268) who acknowledges the option to consider, in addition to animals and plants, non living parts of environments ε   as "physical processes, artifacts, images, and other forms of beings." Nι   of the categories in Descola's list is really inclusive of planets, stars, constellations, or any *thing* not on Earth. These items could be added to Descola's list of items with which humans interact and toward which I shift our focus of analysis, and/or they can be lumped together into categories which can then be added to Descola's list. Possible labels for categories that would include planets, stars, and constellations, and other *objects* outside of Earth's atmosphere are: celestial bodies, extraterrestrial beings, space objects, and astronomical objects. These *objects* lie outside of Earth's atmosphere, but they influence Earth and its inhabitants in profound ways. Analyzing the correspondences (Ingold 2013) between these *objects* and Earth's inhabitants is thus a productive exercise.

My strategy for elaborating upon the idea of a biosocial universe is two-fold. First, I describe the recognition by Kodi people of the biosocial character of the universe. The "particular social forms" (Descola 2013: 232) that the Kodi collective projects to entities beyond the Earth constitute the universe as a biosocial world. I use the Kodi cosmology here for practical reasons; namely, because I have conducted approximately fifteen months of field work in Kodi since 1997 and it is the ethnographic situation that I know best. In fact, I selected the particular theoretical frames that I use here in this chapter because they work well in explaining the ethnographic phenomena of Kodi. Moreover, my contributions to these theories are actually Kodi people's ideas, or at least my interpretations of them.

For the second strategy, I describe the universe as seen through the culture of science, especially the disciplines of astronomy, physics, and astrophysics, which projects their own culturally specific meanings onto astronomical objects. In scientists' collective cosmology is the universe biosocial? Do scientists think of the universe and its constituents as engaging in biosocial relationships? Evaluating similarities and differences in an Indigenous cosmology and a scientific cosmology reveals insights into the ecology of the universe and expands theoretical musings on naturecultures. Finding patterns in knowledge across cultures may reveal aspects of human bodies' correspondences with celestial bodies that transcend social constructs, and that lie in the realm of independent reality (Barad 2007). The type of extralinguistic reality (Barad 2007) I wish to identify is not only one related to material nature but also one related to an anthropological biosocial becoming (Ingold and Palsson 2013).

This analytical adventure serves the purpose of finding out how broad the concept of biosocial can be, of seeing how far out into space the human-nonhuman biosocial strings are attached. Researchers such as Hartigan (2015: 2) engage in "rethinking sociality by following examples of culture across species lines." My twist on the multispecies trend is to build an even more inclusive model of society by following examples of sociality across the living-nonliving barrier. I deal with abiotic natural entities in contrast to non-living, man-made materials as, for example, Jane Bennett (2010) does with metal, trash, and landfills. This is a notable contrast because I wish to use this exercise to expand taxonomies by lifting off the lid on conventional biological taxonomy and adding abiotic natural taxa. The expanded taxonomy includes multiple ranks of taxa populated by celestial bodies—one for planets, one for stars, one for satellites, etc.—and the aggregate rank "astronomical object." A taxonomist working with this classification would find the social in it by studying the relationships among taxa. This is a post-biology style of taxonomy, or, in the case where the taxonomist is working with folk taxonomies, the endeavor is post-ethnobiology.

A hierarchical taxonomy of astronomical bodies already exists within the science of astronomy. The observable universe, whose edge is 46.6 billion light years away, consists of superclusters of galaxies containing sub-clusters made up of groups of galaxies within which are subgalaxies that subsume solar systems that contain planets, stars, and other matter. By the definition of astronomy, the observable universe includes all of the objects whose light could potentially reach an observer on Earth, regardless of the observer's location and use of technology. From a social scientist's point of view, though, the positionality of the observer is tremendously influential on what light-emitting objects she witnesses. An observer's witnessing of light depends on social factors such as geography, class, gender, access to viewing instruments as well as to personal factors such as interest and eyesight. Culture, of course, also conditions what a person observes and how they interpret what they "see." This is exceedingly clear in the different interpretations of the astronomical objects that are the subjects of this chapter.

Taking account of the subjectivity involved in observing empirical objects leads us to consider how entities become social or loose sociality as well as how social worlds form and change. Objects in the observable universe come into focus; for example, when our attention is directed to them, or when viewing instruments are accessible. Objects go out of focus too because our attention is diverted, or because the expanding universe or the own object's death causes their light to no longer reach Earth. The ability to observe—or taking the opportunity to observe—an astronomical object is not a necessary condition for it to be part of our biosocial world. This is true for astronomical objects, although it may or may not be true for all materials. In the case of astronomical objects, they influence us regardless of our cultural recognition of their bearing on our lives. This is one of the reasons why astronomical objects are so compelling for anthropologists who study human-environment interactions: because they influence our biosocial becomings (Ingold and Palsson 2013) in the presence or absence of our cultural constructions or our collective consciousness.

Of the enormous number of objects in the observable universe that are potentially available for study, I choose to focus on only two astronomical objects: the Moon and the Sun. These are two especially meaningful objects for Kodi people. The Moon and the Sun receive the bulk of the attention in this chapter as a reflection of the attention they receive in Kodi culture. Kodi and astronomers alike can, of course, observe more objects than just these two. In addition, those privileged persons who have access to high-powered viewing instruments can "see" a tremendous number of objects. But this small selection of merely two astronomical bodies is grounded in the ethnographic data from Kodi.

COMPARING SPECULATIONS ABOUT SPACE-TIME IN TWO CULTURES

In what ways do dynamic biosocial interactions between Earthbound and extraterrestrial subjects coproduce biosocial change on Sumba? Where the Earth, Moon, and Sun perform their own orbital dynamics relative to one another, humans on Earth interpret the visible aspects of the celestial bodies' characters into space-time cultures. Some humans, namely astronomers, listen to the universe with high-tech gravitational wave detectors that enable them to hear the gravitational waves "generated by binary supermassive black holes, ultra-compact binaries, and small black holes falling into supermassive black holes" (Haynes and Betz 2016: 27). Other humans, namely the Kodi people, may not be able to listen to gravitational waves, but their ritual technologies enable them to hear the Moon and Sun. The components of space-time cultures where the Earth, Moon, and Sun appear are fundamental to human worlds. They relate to when and where to wake, sleep, reproduce, gather with whole clans, disperse into sublineages, produce or procure food, worship, heal, and do other things. The entanglements are pervasive and profound. These explorations of the entanglements between the nonliving and living, Earthlings and Space-lings cast the spotlight on their biosocial relationships by especially considering kinship, sickness, healing, death, and the afterlife.

Speculations about the agency of astronomical objects are not outside of the realm of either Indigenous knowledge, or scientific astronomy, or anthropology. In all three systems of knowledge, we humans speculate about the compositions, activities, and intentions of astronomical objects, but we also depend upon on empirical observations of the lights and sounds that astronomical objects generate. Astronomy differs from Indigenous knowledge and cultural anthropology in that it combines experimentation and mathematics with observation, speculation, and theorization. Sometimes the lights and sounds are empirically observed and sometimes they are inferred. In the Indigenous realm, an example of inferred knowledge is when Marapu elders, healers, and priests have conversations with the Moon and Sun. The Marapu specialists speak to celestial bodies, and they hear or see them speak back. An example of empiricism as the basis of knowledge is when astronomers conceptualize their interactions with astronomical objects in similar ways as Kodi do, but they rely on nonhuman sensing equipment. Physicists devote their lives to developing instruments like the Laser Interferomenter Gravity-wave Observatory (LIPO) that enhance their abilities to discover what the universe has to tell them. LIPO enables researchers to, for instance, "pick out the voice of cosmic gravity from the static of earthly mumblings" (Haynes and Betz 2016: 26).

Physicists continue to speculate on the characteristics and causes of gravitational waves as, looking towards the future, they search for quieter places to listen for cosmic gravity's voices, and develop new instruments in hopes of more clearly hearing more voices. Speculation got physicists to the point where Einstein and his successors imagined gravitational waves, debated whether they existed, kept searching for them, built instruments to detect them, and finally recorded gravitational waves with LIPO for the first time in September 2015. If speculation about the agency of celestial bodies is good enough for physicists, it is good enough for Indigenous peoples and perhaps for anthropologists as well. The universe contains more information we do not yet know than what we have already discovered, and speculation might help us imagine the not-yet-observable. Martin Hewitson from the European Space Agency said, "We've only been looking at the universe with our eyes, but we've never heard the universe before September 2015. It looks impressive, but imagine when you start listening" (quoted in Haynes and Betz 2016).

Do Kodi people attempt to adopt the perspectives of astronomical objects as a method for listening to the universe? Kodi people have been listening to in addition to looking at the Moon and Sun for many generations. Looking and listening help Kodi people adopt the Moon's and Sun's perspectives and translate their compositions, activities, and functions in numerous ways.

Kodi people interpret misfortunes as messages from the Moon and Sun. Marapu diviners use divination to hear what the Moon and Sun are saying. Kodi healers, their patients, and the patients' families consider the illness outcomes to symbolize the emotions of the Moon and Sun. Where multispecies ethnographers and posthuman theorists encourage researchers to search for nonhumans' "dispositions, motivations, and intentions" (Kohn 2007: 5), Kodi people already perceive celestial bodies to be fully realized selves. The Kodi understanding of the world and how to make it are evident in the meanings Kodi people assign to astronomical beings.

A key difference between what Kodi and what physicists hear from celestial bodies is that Kodi hear beings who have consciousness. The Moon and Sun think, emote, and talk like people. They tell people whether they are angry or satisfied, hungry or satiated. The astronomical objects embody speaking souls who tell Kodi the causes of their illnesses and misfortunes, and how to heal their problems. The Moon and Sun tell Kodi where displaced souls are or are not; how many chickens, pigs, and water buffalo to sacrifice; which plant medicines treat sick persons' ailments; when to perform healing, soul retrieval rituals and whether or not the rites were successful; and when to perform funeral rites and whether or not the dead souls are at rest.

When astronomers listen to the cosmos, they hear very different things than Kodi people do. Astrophysicists cannot hear what Kodi hear because they lack socialization in Marapu rituals and beliefs. Vice versa, Kodi cannot hear what physicists hear because they lack scientific training and do not have access to tools like LIPO that revolutionize human's sensing of outer space. Where Marapu priests hear embodied souls with human-like voices that speak an extraordinary language, scientists hear the sounds made by aurora, meteors, gravitational waves, "ripples in the curvature of space-time" (Eicher 2016a: 6), and, in the case of the event that LIPO heard, collisions of massive (twenty-nine and thirty-six solar masses) and distant (1.3 billion light years) black holes. The sounds of these astronomical events sound like screams, chirps, cracklings, booms, whistling, hums, and even silence (Eicher 2016a; Eicher 2016b; Haynes and Betz 2016; O'Meara 2016). Scientists bring very different worldviews to their listening events than Kodi do. Where Kodi approach celestial bodies as though they were selves, physicists approach them as though they were objects. While astronomers speak of the "cosmic voice" (O'Meara 2016: 20), they think of the cosmos's voice as a metaphor for the human voice. When Kodi hear and talk to the Moon and the Sun, the souls in those bodies have human voices.

Humans in the two groups I deal with see themselves as living in the same space-time as astronomical objects. Scientists know the astronomical objects share with humans the characteristic of having biophysical "bodies," but differ from humans in not being alive and being in distant locations. Marapu believers think of astronomical bodies as locations also. For astronomers, the Moon is a place where living humans can and have visited, but they know the Sun is too hot for humans. Marapu believers know both the Moon and Sun as locations where living humans should not go, although the "sick" souls of humans, plants, and animals who are in the transitional state between living and nonliving might unfortunately go. The Moon and Sun are locations where previously living, previously human spirits stay who exhibit routine behaviors. They are similar to humans, yet much more powerful as evidenced by their brilliant light and intense heat in the case of the Sun.

I follow the premise that enchanted and disenchanted worldviews are complementary in the sense that comparing the Kodi supposedly encha d view with the scientific supposedly disenchanted view expands anth pology's contribution to academic dialogues about ecology, humanity, science, and philosophy. Considering some similarities and differences between astronomers' and Kodi understandings of the Sun and Moon demonstrates that human bodies evolve in relation to celestial bodies. The world beyond Earth has profound significance in human lives. The meanings humans assign to celestial bodies and the desire to know celestial bodies comprises relationships among humans and between humans and nonhumans. Humans feel compelled to engage in social relationships with celestial bodies because we recognize that we live in biosocial worlds, though we vary cross-culturally in the ways we acknowledge and express our recognition.

POSITIONING AND UN-GROUNDING BODIES IN SPACE-TIME

Celestial bodies are "*parts* of human society" (Knight 2005: 1). Celestial bodies are parts of human bodies in every sense: biophysically, socially, culturally, mentally, emotionally, and spiritually. Celestial bodies, like consummately social human bodies, make their worlds, in part, by negotiating their positions in space-time. Actants move through space-time relative to other actants as part of their existence as social beings. Analyzing actants' positions in space-time is a method for understanding those actants as social beings in a vast universe. Where do human bodies and celestial bodies position themselves relative to one another? How and why do bodies position themselves in space-time in their particular ways? These are human questions asked by humans in their quests to know the universe; Indigenous people ask them, astronomers ask them, and anthropologists ask them.

The ways human communities ask and answer questions about the space-time positionings of their world's beings make evident those communities' biosocial constructions of the world. In this chapter, I have described Kodi

knowledge about the relationships between Earthly and extraterrestrial subjects and subsequently discussed that knowledge relative to scientific knowledge in the discipline of astronomy. The subject of this chapter follows from
the grounded exploration of human-seaworm relations in the preceding chapters and elevates our attention skyward, toward human relations with entities
outside of the Earth's atmosphere. The analysis of extraterrestrial beings
shifts the *field* from Earth's surface to the spaces beyond Earth. The *sky* is
the field site. In un-grounding—narratively but not theoretically—the ethnographic content, this chapter disrupts the Earth-centric tendencies of conventional studies of anthropogenic environmental change. Where this book's
ɪ ᵓding chapters were informed by marine ecology, this chapter draws from
th. ᵓences of astronomy, physics, and astrophysics. Integrating information
from these other scholarly fields enhances the ethnographic information that
I have collected myself or borrowed from other ethnographers who have
worked on Sumba. In the real world, moreover, Earthly systems are integrated
with celestial systems which are integrated with terrestrial systems which
are integrated with aquatic ecosystems (Menge et al. 2009). While one sole
anthropologist cannot become expert in the many disciplines that can potentially inform ethnographic data, she can draw on those sciences to connect
the constitution and behavior of nature's constituents with one another and
thus to enrich what we know about the composition, structure, and function
of ecosystems as well as change dynamics in ecosystems.

This analysis needs both anthropology and astronomy to be effective
since the Moon and Sun are as much social subjects as they are astronomical
objects. Their roles in human lives are constructed in biosocial contexts relative to Earth and Earthbound beings. That is true for their roles in Kodi lives
as well as their roles in astronomers' lives. In the processes of constructing
their meanings from their situated positions, humans fold the Moon and Sun
into their biosocial worlds and work them into what it means to be human.
Reciprocally, celestial bodies encircle humans with a much more spacious
biosocial universe by pulling, pushing, illuminating, darkening, heating,
and through additional forces enacted upon the Earth and the bodies, minds,
hearts, and spirits of humans.

Chapter 5

Listening for Cosmic Voices and Speculating about Their Perspectives

KODI PEOPLE'S ENTANGLEMENTS WITH ASTRONOMICAL OBJECTS

What are the "particular social forms" (Descola 2013: 232) that Kodi culture projects onto the universe? This is a question about how humans make the biosocial worlds that extend beyond Earth's boundaries, and to answer it this chapter takes on the task of assessing Kodi people's knowledge about the objects in their sky and their practices related to cosmic bodies. Kodi people factor material information and symbolic meanings from the Moon and Sun into their conceptualizations of and practices in space-time.

Being Kodi, being human always involves co-belonging in the same universe as cosmic agents. The lives of Earthly humans and nonhumans are entangled with cosmic agents. While many astronomical objects are actors in Kodi's biosocial worlds, the Moon and the Sun are especially active agents in the Kodi universe as indicated by their being the ones people most frequently evoke. Through thinking, expressing, and acting out their cosmology, Kodi share their world with these two especially prominent subjects/objects in the sky.

The question of whether the Moon, Sun, and other cosmic bodies are more accurately referred to as "objects" or "subjects" is tricky to answer because in Kodi cosmology the sky-beyond-Earth is inhabited by objects with "dispositions, motivations, and intentions" (Kohn 2007: 5). In possessing these qualities, the Moon and Sun are *selves* in a similar sense as seaworms are *selves*. Kodi people communicate information about the "dispositions, motivations, and intentions" (Kohn 2007: 5) of the Moon and Sun in various everyday and ritual contexts. In rituals, they chant the names of cosmic companions in rhythmic couplets, sing to them, play music for them, offer sacrifices to them, and divine their feelings while coaxing them into feeling and behaving in desirable ways. In everyday situations, Kodi people recount the histories of the Moon and Sun in myths and stories, and describe their own and their loved ones' encounters with the cosmic actants.

The Moon and Sun have "traditional" Kodi monikers as well as common everyday names. *Wulla* is the everyday name for the Moon. *Lod'do* or *Mata Lod'do* is the Sun's common name. The traditional names of the Moon and Sun are spoken together in this lyrical couplet: *Pati Ndera Wulla Raŋa Horo Lod'do*. This name identifies the Moon Sun as a complementary pair that includes a female side, *Pati Ndera Wulla*, and a male side, *Raŋa Horo Lod'do*. *Pati Ndera* is an iconic name for Kodi people; usually women, but also some men. *Raŋa Horo* is an iconic name given to Kodi men. These human names were taken and given to the Moon and Sun, or vice versa. The Moon Sun is a double-gendered or transgendered subject. S/he belongs to the same taxonomic class as Mother Seaworm Father Fish (*Inya Nale Bapa Ipu Mbaha*), Mother Guardian of the Earth Father Guardian of the Rivers (*Inya Mangu Tana Bapa Mangu Loko*), and Great Mother Great Father (*Inya Bokolo Bapa Bokolo*). Members of this class occupy the top of the supernatural hierarchy. These are the deities who oversee the cosmos (*Pati Ndera Wulla Raŋa Horo Lod'do*), the Earth (Mother Guardian of the Earth Father Guardian of the Rivers), oceans (Mother Seaworm Father Fish), and who are the progenitors of all beings (Great Mother Great Father).

The Moon Sun in Kodi cosmology support humans and nonhuman beings in life and in death. This principle of mutual support appears in Kodi beliefs about death and the afterlife. The following abbreviated version of the lunar cycles myth is foundational to the Kodi cosmology.

> The brothers Magilo and Pokilo, our ancient ancestors, caught the Moon in their hunting net. Magilo and Poliko released the Moon into the sea because the Moon would never be able to shine again if it was captured in their net. With no moonlight, people would not dance or sing. If the brothers had kept the Moon tied up in their net, we would have no moonlight to guide the way when we are out walking through the countryside at night. With no Moon, people would not be able to pray to the Moon's spirit. The Moon's spirit is the one who cares for our children, keeps them healthy, and restores their health when they are sick. The spirit in the Moon is the one who provides us with food, who protects our families, and who restores our plants and animals when they suffer.

This myth illustrates Kodi ideas about the relationships between humans and the Moon both now and in the past. The lunar cycles myth expresses the perception that the Moon and humans are mutually constituted via assistance with reproduction and food. In the myth of the Moon's cycles, the brothers volley the Moon into its cycles of death and rebirth while the Moon supports human conception and development. The Moon and people, especially females, follow parallel rhythms.

The celestial body is the capturable part of the Moon. The body is the one that humans sense through sight. They know it from seeing it regularly as it rises out of the ocean. Kodi know the Moon as a material object comparable to other physical beings that they can capture in their nets, like pigs or macaques. Only, the Moon is much more valuable and is one of a kind. There is only one Moon body for the Moon spirit to inhabit, while there are many bodies for the pig and macaque spirits to inhabit. In its singularity, the Moon has tremendous influence on humans. The Moon spirit and humans engage in reciprocal relations, where the Moon gives medicine, food, and light, people reciprocate with song and dance. Singing and dancing are euphemisms for the healing (*yaigho*) ceremonies which are one of the major types and most frequently performed rituals in Kodi social life. Singing and dancing references the social lives of Kodi when kin and allies gather to collectively support sick, dying, or dead members of their social groups. The Moon is an important attendee and agent at these ceremonies. The Moon belongs to the social collective.

THE SUN AND MOON ARE LIFE AND DEATH

The Moon communicates its "dispositions, motivations, and intentions" (Kohn 2007: 5) to humans through its behaviors, including through its regular monthly cycles as well as in its other periodic apparitions. Kodi conceptualize the lunar cycle as beginning with birth, starting off as a small sliver, going through a waxing period, becoming full, going through a waning period, becoming smaller or darker, and then dying. Like people, the Moon goes through a birth-death cycle. The Moon repeatedly reincarnates. Kodi describe at least ten phases of the Moon (Hoskins 1993), which are listed here in order from the first quarter Moon to the new Moon (Hoskins 1993):

Kodi Name of the Moon Phase	Literal Translation in English
Pa ice baŋga	Dogs see the Moon [First Quarter Moon]
Wulla muda	Young Moon
Taŋara binye	Moon seen over the village gate
Wulla nja ndaha	No-good Moon
Wulla mburu manu	Falling Chicken Moon [Waxing Moon]
Wulla taru or *Taru rara*	Full Moon or Red Full Moon
Wulla malupu, wulla malaka	Old Moon, Skinny Moon [Waning Moon]

Kodi Name of the Moon Phase	**Literal Translation in English**
Maŋga la panuna	Waiting on the plateau
Piri hyudo na kapandu taruhinikya	Several nights of darker Moons
Wulla pa palu muŋgo	Ceremonial Moon
Mati wulla	Dead Moon [New Moon]

The Moon's phases are symbolically aligned with cycles of danger, love, and safety. The waxing Moon is associated with danger, death, and taboos on rituals. Homicides are more likely to occur when the upper horn of the young crescent Moon aligns with other bright celestial bodies. Nighttime rendezvous, love, sex, and conception tend to occur during the full Moon. This idea may reference a belief that women's cycles of ovulation and menstruation are synchronized with lunar cycles. The waning Moon is thought of as a safer time of the month. Taboos on rituals and on ritual speech are lifted during the waning phase.

The Seaworm Priest from Bukubani says, "When the Moon is growing, we wait in silence. When the Moon is already past full, we feel free to talk about *patana* (tradition)."

The Seaworm Priest's point aligns with the scheduling of the seaworm harvesting ritual seven days following the full Moon in the Big Seaworm Month.

Eclipses are symbolized differently from the Moon's phases, but are still symbolized as dangerous or safe, life or death. The Moon's eclipse foreshadows death while the Sun's eclipse foreshadows birth. Kodi people interpret an eclipse of the Moon to mean that either a murderer intends to commit a homicide, or a pregnant woman will miscarry.

Murders and miscarriages "always happen when the Moon eclipses," according to one Kodi man.

An eclipse of the Sun means a great prophet has arisen in Indonesia or somewhere in the world. The Moon points to murderers, the Sun points to visionaries. Prophets are intermediaries between the human and supernatural worlds, between Earthbound beings and non-Earthbound beings. Murderers are sort of intermediaries too since their actions send souls—the souls of people who die "bad" deaths from murder or miscarriage—to the Moon and Sun. These conditions tell us that the Moon, Sun, and humans have profound relationships with both living humans and dead ancestors.

The Moon and Sun supervise crucial phenomena in the cosmos. The presence of the Moon and Sun is equivalent to the availability of land and water, seaworms and fish. Life and death hinge upon these basic necessities. The Moon and Sun are intimately involved with life, death, and the states in between. The Moon and Sun are powerful personalities and they are also pivotal locations. As geographic locations, the Moon and Sun are accessible places. They are the places of refuge for the souls of all beings whose souls are out of place. When souls are in the "right" locations in the sense of being where they choose to be, the world is "right," meaning that its inhabitants are healthy and functioning well. When souls are displaced, the world is not "right." Displaced souls cause illness in human and nonhuman beings, and can cause disease and death in animals, plants, and people as well as environmental disasters.

The fate of souls after life depends on the conditions of their deaths, on whether the deaths were "good" or "bad." In "good" deaths, a person dies a peaceful death in old age. The loved ones of the dead gently usher these peaceful souls out of their bodies over the course of a series of funeral rites that can last days and even years and that are performed in the dead people's homes and in clan-based cemeteries. Inlanders practice primary and secondary bur s. Deceased bodies are buried in tombs in the central courtyards of inland h   lets as their primary burials. Their remains are later moved to megalithic gravesites in the Great Clan Villages for their secondary burials. In "bad" deaths, a person dies unexpectedly or too young due to diseases or accidents. The dead's kin do not have the opportunity to usher their souls peacefully into the afterlife because these distraught souls flee to the Moon and Sun. The major ritual obligation of the still-living in these "bad" death cases is to summon the dead person's soul back to Earth before hosting the multiday and multiyear funeral rites. Loved ones attempt to retrieve these displaced souls from the Moon and Sun through *yaigho* rituals, or else risk suffering from disease and death themselves.

RITUALS FOR SOULS WHO ESCAPE TO THE MOON SUN

Yaigho are soul retrieval rituals performed when souls fly away to the Moon Sun. In Marapu, "souls inhabit all beings," according to Radu Kaka. "All beings who have souls are human-like. Humans have souls, and so do snakes, trees, rice, maize, chili peppers . . ."

In addition to these living nonhumans, nonliving nonhumans have souls. Rocks and mountains, for example, have souls. *Yaigho* rituals are not necessary to retrieve all beings' souls, but *yaigho* is necessary for displaced human souls and ancestors' souls. As mentioned previously, humans' living souls need to be retrieved when they die young, when accidents cause their deaths, and when a murderer kills them. Dead humans' souls need to be retrieved when the nonhuman entities they embody "die." Examples are when wildfires burn immature rice; when maize still growing in gardens burns in wildfires; and when people desecrate the embodiments of powerful ancestors, such as rocks or trees. When displaced souls need to be retrieved, people summon *toyo yaigho* (*yaigho* officiants) and a team of ritual specialists to lead them and their extended families through *yaigho* ceremonies. They stage their *yaigho* ceremonies at several key religious sites. Two key locations in *yaigho* rituals are the *Mori Cana* and the *Marapu Binye*.

Mori Cana and *Marapu Binye* are two main ceremonial spaces in all inland patriclans' hamlets (*kalimbiatu*). The spirits of the patriclans' hamlets' founding ancestors—the first settlers—inhabit the *Mori Cana* and *Marapu Binye*. These altars themselves possess souls, like all of the other major types of altars (see Tables 5.1 and 5.2) that structure the Kodi landscape (Fowler 1999). The two are related as kin, where *Mori Cana* is the older brother and *Marapu Binye* is the younger sister. The founding ancestors are conceptualized as having been two siblings, a pair whose male-female aspects express an ethic of gender complementarity. The *Mori Cana* and *Marapu Binye* ʾ ʾar to us in our everyday vision as each consisting of a tree and a rock cᴜ.   The trees for the *Mori Cana* and the *Marapu Binye* are one of three specific species: either *ronggo kodi* (*Bombax ceiba* L. Malvaceae), or *ronggo dawa* (*Ceiba pentandra* (L.) Gaertn. Malvaceae), or *kawongo* (*Hibiscus tiliaceus* L. Malvaceae) trees. The rocks that make up the cairns are where other ancestors' spirits sit for visits with the progenitors' spirits.

The *Mori Cana* has a powerful soul, he is the patriarchal figure, the "one who blesses us, who cools us off, and who thereby enables us to become human," as the young Kodi woman Lidia puts it.

Table 5.1   Altars in the Kodi Landscape Listed in Order of the Sequential Performance of Harvest Rituals

Name of the Altar	Location of the Altar	Materials Used to Make the Altar	Social Role of the Altar Spirit
Wild Taboo Altar (*Kahale Liang Hari*)	border zones: gardens/forests or gardens/ grasslands	rock and wooden stick	manager of gardens
Spirit Source (*Mata Marapu*)	Household	wooden shelf	guard of household; residence of Great Mother Great Father
Lord of the Land (*Mori Cana*)	garden hamlet	rock and tree (*Hibiscus tiliaceus, Bombax ceiba,* or *Ceiba pentandra*)	supervisor of patriclan lands; residence of Mother of the Land Father of the Rivers; son of *Watu Kareka;* deputy to *Marapu Mu Toyo*
Gate Spirit (*Marapu Binye*)	front entrance of garden hamlet	rock and wooden post or tree	prevents evil spirits and disease from entering hamlet; sister of *Mori Cana*
Human Eating Spirit (*Marapu Mu Toyo*)	ancestral village	rock and tree (*kapiha*)	master of patriclan and all land that belongs to it

Table 5.2   Altars in the Kodi Landscape Listed in Order of the Sequential Performance of Planting Rituals

Name of the Altar	Location of the Altar	Materials Used to Make the Altar	Social Role of the Altar Spirit
Lord of the Land (*Mori Cana*)	garden hamlet	rock and tree (*Hibiscus tiliaceus, Bombax ceiba,* or *Ceiba pentandra*)	guard of household; residence of Great Mother Great Father; son of *Watu Kareka*; deputy of *Marapu Mu Toyo*
Sub-clan ritual house (*umma*)	ritual house in the garden hamlet	various types of timber trees	protector of the *umma*, a segment of a patriclan or patrilineage
Seat of the Seeds (*Palondo Wini*)	center of garden	rock, dibble sticks, and split bamboo culms	sacrificial altar of Biri Koni, the rice spirit
Stone Shelter (*Watu Kareka*)	edge of garden	rock and dibble sticks	guards the garden from evil, disease, and pests; symbolizes Lady Kenggor, mother of Biri Koni, *Marapu Binye, Mori Cana,* etc.
Spirit Source (*Mata Marapu*)	household	wooden shelf	guard of household; residence of Great Mother—Great Father

The *Mori Cana* shelters the entire hamlet, making it a safe and welcoming place for the ancestors' spirits as well as the living humans. The hamlet's residents reciprocate through various forms of caretaking: praying to the ancestors, offering first fruits of harvests (*hangapung* or *padolo*), pruning the tree, arranging the rocks, and otherwise protecting the altar. In their prayers, living people say "thank you" and "please" to show their gratitude for what the *Mori Cana* provides and to ask him for what they need. An example comes from Galu Hangoko Hamlet where, on March 22, 1998, Lidia performed *hangapung*. She roasted a sacrificial chicken for the *Mori Cana* and hung two pairs of ripe rice inflorescences from the tree's branches on the day prior to harvesting the bulk of her rice crop. Lidia said this to her "*ambu mati* (dead grandparents)":

Jangan kasih kurang	Don't give us an insufficient harvest
Supaya tetap banyak[1]	So that we continuously have plenty
Ang ela mati ambu	The dead grandparents are here
Nduke monno tomu	You came to be with your offspring
Amba waŋyo wawi	Grandmother we offer you this pig
Hiyo Ambiapa	Here grandfather

Ang diya binyana mori	You are the true lord
Monno ama dinya mori	And you are the real lord
Ban pa mariŋgi	Cool us with your blessings
Pama lala ghaiyo mori	Smelt us into humans
Yo Marapu Bokolo	You are the Great Spirit
Wondo kapambal ana minye ana mone	Fill your daughters' and sons' stomachs

In her prayer, Lidia hybridizes *Mori Cana* by combining elements of Marapu with hints of Christianity. "Marapu Bokolo" literally translates as "Great Spirit" or "Big Spirit" and Lidia addresses him as a god-like figure would appear in a monotheistic religion—as the "real lord." Yet, Lidia also affectionately addresses her ancestors *amba* (grandmothers), *ambiapa* (grandfathers), and *ambu* (grandparents) who are members of the *marapu* (ancestors) taxa in the polytheistic Marapu religion. Lidia calls on "all my relations"—to borrow a Lakota form of addressing the spirits (*Mitakuye oyasin* in Lakota) and expressing ideas about the interconnectedness of people, animals, plants, and so forth—for support and provision.

A key role of the *Mori Cana* is to fetch the souls of the prematurely dead and the accidentally killed from the Moon Sun. Sometimes the souls of the *Mori Cana* themselves fly away to the Moon Sun, and have to be retrieved. The *Mori Cana* are the ones who bring displaced souls back down to Earth and back home to their hamlets. If the *Mori Cana* did not perform this role, then the peace and wellbeing that ideally exists when all souls are in their places could not be restored to the Earthbound world. The *Mori Cana* stands in the center of hamlets with all residents' houses clustered around them.

The *Marapu Binye* stands beside the hamlets' main entrances, and is conceptualized as a sort of gate to the hamlet. The traditional name of the *Marapu Binye* Spirit is *Kawoŋgo Mbali Binye Ɖgalu Wallu Kari* (*Hibiscus Guarding the Door Erythrina Fencing the Enclosure*). The *Marapu Binye*'s role is to guard the hamlets' gates and to regulate who/what comes and goes. She also has many other roles: (1) as the filter to keep bad spirits and diseases from entering hamlets; (2) as the ritual site for cleansing hamlets of thievery and sin; and (3) as the site for ritual sacrifices when souls come back down to Earth from the Moon Sun.

The *yaigho* officiant for Magho Kawongo Hamlet further explained *Marapu Binye*'s latter role when he said, "When I have to retrieve the souls of a murder victim, a woman who died during childbirth because her baby was dead in her belly, rice that burned in the field, the spirit of a sick person, or the spirit of a dead person, I play music and sing to the *Marapu Binye*. I have to offer sacrificed chickens to the *Marapu Binye* to convince her to open the hamlet gate so the descending souls can re-enter the hamlet."

The *Marapu Binye* is a fierce defender of the wellbeing of her loved ones, but sometimes diseases slip through her filters and cause the residents of her hamlet to fall ill. While illnesses weaken bodies, they also threaten souls. When people are sick, their souls might "escape," a threat that often initiates a *yaigho* performance. *Yaigho* are a means for preventing soul "escape" before people die, as well as the aforementioned method for retrieving souls from the Moon Sun after bodies die.

ANCESTORS' SOULS RETREAT TO THE MOON SUN WHEN RICE AND MAIZE BURN

The dead bodies for whom *yaigho* are performed may be those of humans or nonhuman beings. The great efforts devoted to performing *yaigho* for souls who escape to the Sun and Moon indicates the great importance of trees, rice, livestock, wild animals, and other creatures who have great value in people's foodways. People's relationships with the Sun and Moon mediate their relationships with the animals and plants that are vital to their subsistence systems. Their relationships with the Sun and Moon are also expressions of ideas about vitality.

The souls of two of the specific cultivated plants growing in Kodi vegetable gardens contain souls that flee to the Moon Sun when the grains are unjustly or prematurely killed as, for example, happens when they are burned up in wildfires.

Hona Tiela describes the "escape" of the soul of *ŋgaga-wotoro* (rice-maize) when it burns as, "rising up like the fire's smoke."

The souls of rice-maize, "run to the Sun because the plants originate from a human and therefore have a soul," the Kodi woman Rutta Raddu Palla explains. "We must *yaigho* if the souls of rice and maize escape to the Moon because her soul is a human one."

Rice and maize are coupled here in Rutta Raddu Palla's explanation as one rice-maize entity. The conceptualization of rice-maize as a dead human's soul is illustrated in the Biri Koni myth which tells the story about the young girl, Biri Koni, whose body transformed into rice-maize and several other garden crops when her father sacrificed her in the garden (Fowler 1999). Biri Koni's soul is still present in the world. She and other dead human's souls are part of the living human's society.

Kodi deeply value having strong relationships with dead humans, and they work hard to stay on good terms with their ancestors. The *yaigho* to bring the rice-maize soul back to Earth is typically scheduled for one, two, or three years following the wildfire event that killed the rice-maize. *Yaigho*-ing is one forum for renegotiating people's relationships with their ancestors' spirits when something goes wrong.

Hona Tiela stresses the importance of performing *yaigho* after a rice-maize garden burns when he says, "The owner of the garden may be sick if his garden burns. We *yaigho* so the owner will not be sick anymore. If we do not *yaigho*, the owner may die."

Some *yaigho* serve multiple purposes. An example is when a family in a small inland hamlet staged a *yaigho* to both heal one of their sick members and to retrieve Biri Koni's blackened soul.

Muda Duni, who was the *toyo yaigho* on that occasion on June 13, 2007, said that his clients held the *yaigho* because, "They didn't want her [the sick woman's] soul to escape to the Sun and Moon. And they needed to bring the rice's soul back to the Earth."

The June 13, 2007 *yaigho* had the dual purpose of prevention and retrieval. The retrieval attempt was for the soul of rice—who is the little girl, Biri Koni—that wildfire destroyed. In the garden of the same family to which the sick person belonged, what started out as an unthreatening cooking fire turned into a fast-moving wildfire when the wind picked up, stoked the flames, and carried the fire across the landscape (see Fowler 2013 for a longer version of this story). The burning flames caused the nearly ripened rice's soul to escape its bodies and fly away to the Moon Sun. So, the family hosted the *yaigho* in the hopes of bringing Biri Koni's soul back to the Earth. The displacement of the rice's soul, the sickness of the rice grower's body, and the risk of her soul escaping are connected, of course, through etiology: destructive fires in a family's garden cause the displacement of burned plants' souls that, in turn, cause illness.

To affect healing in the living body of the sick human and in the transspecies human-botanical scorched body of Biri Koni, the June 13 *yaigho* performers attempted to cleanse the rice spirit by spraying coconut water up into the air while saying prayers. The host family sacrificed a pig and chicken during that *yaigho*. The *toyo parupu kaloro* (diviner) interpreted the chicken's entrails as indicating that the family would, a few months later in the rainy season, have to *yaigho* again and sacrifice a pig in the garden where Biri Koni's body burned. All of these ritual measures are necessary to take in order for the rice to grow again in the next growing season and for the rice grower to survive the ordeal.

A PATRILINEAGE'S SOUL ESCAPES WHEN A FAMILY MEMBER FELL A TREE

When human souls do escape from their sick bodies and flee to the Moon Sun, they force their family members to muster enough resources for a *yaigho*; resources that include compensation for the *yaigho* officiants, food for the feast, and animals (chickens, pigs, water buffalo) to sacrifice for the deities. The attendees at the feast are members of the hosts' *kabisu* (patriclan). Either one patriclan or two or more closely related patriclans within an *uma* (house) *yaigho* together. The hosts' *kabisu* members are important contributors of resources for the *yaigho* as well, including the sacrificial animals, rice, eggs, and water.

The residents of Mogha Kawongo Hamlet performed a *yaigho* after one of the residents cut down the hamlet's *Mori Cana* tree that embodies the patrilineage's ancestor and the hamlet's first settler. The founder's descendant who cut down the *Mori Cana* in Mogha Kawongo Hamlet did so to symbolically display his rejection of Marapu. He cut down this prominent materialization of the native religion when he converted from Marapu to Protestantism. Soon after the tree felling event, disease, death, and environmental disasters began plaguing the feller's family, gardens, animals, and loved ones. The family had already planted a new *kawongo* tree to grow a new *Mori Cana* becaus⸗ ₃o many of them were sick and they were suffering from many other pr⸗ ₋ms within the family. Their illnesses and dysfunctions clearly signified that their actions of converting and felling had offended the ancestors. Moreover, a *toyo parupu kaloro* (diviner) diagnosed the cause of the family's misfortunes as the loss of the *Mori Cana*'s soul.

"The *Mori Cana* was cut down," said the diviner. "Now he wants to come back down from the sky."

The patrilineage's ancestor—the one whose spirit resided in the tree, whose right place is in the *Mori Cana*—had fled to the Moon Sun after his descendant committed the violent act.

To attempt to cure the illnesses plaguing the family in Magho Kawongo Hamlet, the community determined they would need to retrieve the *Mori Cana*'s soul by staging a *yaigho*. So, the community came together on November 24, 1997 for the *yaigho* when the healers convened in the hamlet with the afflicted family and scores of people from their patriclan. The *yaigho* included the sacrifice of a pig and its offering to the *Mori Cana* as well as the sacrificial roasting and offering of a chicken to the *Marapu Binye* so that, if the spirit of the *Mori Cana* descended from the Moon and Sun, it could enter the hamlet.

The *yaigho* officiant explained, "If we *yaigho* we are supposed to kill a chicken for the *Marapu Binye*. We have a hierarchy of sacrificial altars and must follow protocol in making offerings to the ancestors they embody. If we kill a water buffalo [the animal with the most symbolic value] for the *Mori Cana*, we have to kill a pig [a less symbolically valuable animal] for the *Marapu Binye* because the *Marapu Binye* is like the younger sibling, so the *Mori Cana* demands more respect [i.e., via the killing of a more valuable animal]."

That November 24th *yaigho* was the fourth soul retrieval ritual the Magho Kawongo community had staged for the *Mori Cana*. Sometimes one *yaigho* is sufficient for retrieving displaced souls, but this tree's soul was proving to be extraordinarily difficult to win back. Spending limited resources to support the chanting, drumming, gong playing, sacrificing, feasting, and pleading that go on in *yaigho* is no guarantee that displaced souls will return to Earth. The sponsors, performers, and attendees do not find out whether the soul has returned until the end of a long night of performing. In the early morning hours, shortly before dawn, the Marapu elders who are performing the *yaigho* look for the sign of the soul's release. The sign they expect to see when a soul descends from the Moon and Sun to the Earth is a shooting star whose light streaks through the sky as if it were racing toward a desirable place. If no descending light appears, Marapu elders interpret the lack of signs to mean that the soul did not descend. A soul does not descend when the spirits remain ι ·tisfied by all of the *yaigho* performers' offerings and unconvinced of the sι. ˙ty of their remorsefulness. When the spirits refuse to release souls, the ιviarapu elders conclude that they must perform additional *yaigho* in the future, and that, in the meantime, living humans may continue to suffer from illness and misfortune.

Whether or not the soul descends, the appearance of the brilliant planet *Motoromo* (Venus) in the eastern sky signifies the end of the *yaigho*. In the late-night hours of November 24, 1997, the *toyo yaigho* Muda Duni said, "the drumming and chanting will continue throughout the night until dawn—when *Motoromo* [the morning star] rises."

Exchanging ritual currency builds tight inter- and intra-clan networks in Kodi. One of the ways Kodi people mark their ethnic identity as distinct from the neighboring Wejewa ethnic group is by the way members of patriclans contribute resources to their clanmates' expensive rituals, including not only *yaigho* but also house building, marital ceremonies, and funeral rites. After Yustina Ngedo Pandaka died on May 8, 2014, her kinship network showed up with many resources. Six hundred people came to her funeral bearing two massive, old water buffalos, one tremendously fat pig and many smaller pigs, horses, piles of cash, and many lengths of handwoven cloth. Over the course of her seventy-two-year lifespan, Yustina Ngedo Pandaka contributed material valuables to her clanmates' events, and their presentations of wealth at her funeral were acts of reciprocity.

Kodi persons are "ensembles of social relations" (Ingold 2013: 13 quoting Palsson following Marx). As relational beings, they become beings as they move through life and into death with their social relations. The Village Head of Waiholo Village articulates Ingold's—following Palsson, following Marx—understanding of life when he defines what it means to be Kodi as collaborating with kin and allies to produce rites of passage through life. Kodi lives are generated collectively. To build on the ideas of these Indigenous elders and academic scholars, I would like to add that not only living but also nonliving beings are results of their relations. By nonliving beings, I mean more than just the environmental context within which living beings *collectively* evolve but also the contexts within which living and nonliving beings *collaboratively* become.

VENUS IN KODI SPACE-TIME

Kodi people use *Motoromo* (Venus) as a temporal marker to indicate when to schedule the *yaigho*, and at other times for less monumental occasions. Women who live in Tei Kowewar Hamlet, for example, say, "We'll start getting ready when *Motoromo* rises."

These women who are farmers, orchardists, gatherers, and more look for *Motoromo* to rise above the low hills surrounding their valley to decide when to wake up. On market days, they rely on Venus rising to know when to gather their produce, and head off on the long walk to the paved road where they board trucks going to the weekly marketplace so they can sell their produce (see Fowler 2015 for a longer version of these women's stories). Setting off when Venus rises means arriving at the marketplace early enough to sell their goods to eager traders.

The rising of *Motoromo* varies over the course of a single year and from year-to-year (see Table 5.3). The difference in rising times within an annual cycle is apparent from a comparison of the rising and setting of Venus over time. To illustrate the changes over time and how they might impact ritual performances, I compare the rising and setting of Venus in 1980, 1981, 1997, 1998, 2014, and 2015. The years 1980 and 1981 were within the time frame (1979–1981) when Janet Hoskins was doing ethnographic research in Kodi, and when she witnessed the *yaigho* ceremonies that she writes about in "A Life History from Both Sides" (1985), "The Drum is My Shaman, the Spear Guides His Voice" (1988), "From Diagnosis to Performance" (1996), and other publications. The years 1997 and 1998 were when I myself first conducted ethnographic research in Sumba, and when I witnessed *yaigho* ceremonies on October 20, 1997 and November 24, 1997, and when I woke up and traveled to the marketplace with the group of women referencing Venus as a clock on March 6, 1998. The time difference between 1980 and 1997 and between 1981 and 1998 is seventeen years. Thus, I use 2014 and 2015 as referencing these more recent years makes it possible to consider differences in Venus rising at seventeen year intervals. Another reason for choosing 2014 and 2015 is that I was doing research in Kodi during 2014 and working elsewhere in Indonesia in 2015.

Venus became visible at 8:36 am on October 20, 1997 on the *yaigho* stage in Ghuru Ghela Hamlet, which is on the flat coastal plains not far from the ocean.

Table 5.3   Temporal Variations in the Rising Time of Venus for Western Sumba (9.46°S 119.09°E)*

Month and Day	Year	Rising Time	Time Difference in Venus Rising over 35-Day Span (October 20–November 24)	Time Difference in Venus Rising over 137-Day Span (October 20–March 6)	Time Difference of Venus Rising at 17-year Intervals (1980 to 1997, 1981 to 1998, 1997 to 2014, 1998 to 2015)
October 20	1980	3:30 am			
	1997	8:36 am			+306 minutes (5.1 hours)
	2014	5:38 am			−178 minutes (2.9 hours)
November 24	1980	3:39 am	+9 minutes**		
	1997	8:51 am	−15 minutes		+312 minutes (5.2 hours)
	2014	6:05 am	+27 minutes		−166 minutes (2.8 hours)
March 6	1981	5:41 am		+131 minutes	
	1998	3:08 am		−328 minutes (5.5 hours)	−153 minutes (2.55 hours)
	2015	8:13 am		+155 minutes	+305 minutes (5 hours)
June 13	1980	6:37 am			
	1997	7:43 am			+106 minutes (1.8 hours)
	2014	3:51 am			−232 minutes (3.9 hours)

* The source for this data on Venus rising times is Heaven's Above
**The (+) sign means the rising time is later than the point of comparison. The (−) sign means the rising time is earlier than the point of comparison

Thirty-five days later, on November 24, 1997 Venus became visible at around 8:51 am from the *yaigho* grounds in the nearby Magho Kawongo Hamlet, which is also on Kodi's coastal plains. On March 6, 1998, *Motoromo* became visible in the sky above Tei Kowewar Hamlet at 3:08 am, five and a half hours earlier than it had risen 137 days earlier. To compare the time differences in Venus's rising in the 1980s, note that Venus rose at 3:30 am on October 20, 1980, then nine minutes later at 3:39 am on November 24, 1980, and then 131 minutes later at 5:41 am on March 6, 1981. Venus rose above the western Sumba horizon on October 20, 2014 at 5:38 am, then twenty-seven minutes later at 6:05 am on November 24, 2014, at 6:05 am, and then 155 minutes later at 8:13 am on March 6, 2015. For signaling the end of the *yaigho*, the difference in the time when Venus rose between October 20, 1997 and November 24, 1997 was an insignificant nine minutes. On the other hand, the difference in the time when Venus rose between October 20, 1980 and October 20, 1997 was more than five hours, and between October 20, 1997 and October 20, 2014 was almost three hours. Were there to have actually been *yaigho* on October 20, 1980 and 2014 (as there was when I was in Kodi in 1997), those are significant time differences in terms of the energy output required for chanting and drumming (five hours more in 1997 than in 1980 and three hours less in 2014 than in 1997) and the feasting supplies required to host a crowd for what probably would have required serving an additional meal.

The time lag between when the planet rises and when viewers can see it depends on the viewers' location. The time lag is shorter for people who are on the coast, looking eastward out into the ocean and longer for people whose views of the open horizon are blocked by topographical (e.g., mountains), natural (e.g., trees), or built (e.g., buildings) features.

NONHUMANS AND HUMANS HAVE SOULS

The idea that souls flee to the Moon Sun when bodies are unjustly killed or die applies to any of the types of bodies that ancestors' souls inhabit. We have already seen this to be true for trees, but is also applies to other embodied forms, including houses and pythons.

"All creatures, all things that move and that live have spirits," according to Hona Tiela, and elder who lives in Watu Kahale Hamlet. Hona Tiela says, "Only the spirits of those people who were murdered, or of rice and maize that were burned, [or of other creatures who died violently and unexpectedly] flee to the Moon Sun. Not the souls of everyone who dies."

Included in the category of living, moving creatures are houses. "Houses have ghosts and need to be remembered as well," says Hona Tiela. In the case where people's houses burn up in accidental fires, Hona Tiela says, "*Yaigho* are held to make the houses 'cold' again because the house site is 'hot.'" The "cold" and "hot" here refer to humoral concepts related to items being not taboo/cold and taboo/hot.

What is true for the souls of rice-maize, for houses, for *Mori Cana* trees, and for living humans, is also true for snakes, specifically for pythons. The soul who pythons embody is a formerly living human, the Grandfather Python, and he demands respect. A woman in Kalanga Lulu Hamlet whose name is Pati Bebe (echoing "Pati" in the Moon's name) says that pythons are sacred. She uses the common, everyday word *koboko* to talk about pythons in the non-sanctioned context of an informal conversation with me.

Pati Bebe tells me, "*Kaboko* is the one who occupies the *Mori Cana*. When it is planting season or time to go to Pasola, when we go out to trap pig or harvest rice-maize, we always first pay our respects to the *Mori Cana* [one of Grandfather Python's embodiments]."

Pati Bebe points out that the soul of one ancestor is the soul of another ancestor. She says, "The python's soul is the *Hibiscus*'s soul. Snakes are equivalent to trees which are equivalent to people. The bodies of humans, animals, and plants are interchangeable, and they all potentially embody souls." In her brief explication, Pati Bebe provides insight into Kodi cosmology.

Pati Bebe says that she and her clanmates display their respects for their python ancestor by, "honoring the taboo against eating or killing pythons.

If someone were to mistakenly kill a snake, she would become sick, and then we would have to sacrifice a chicken, pig, or water buffalo as a method for begging pardon and seeking forgiveness from the spirits. Even if *kaboko* is killing one of your pigs, or some other valuable asset, and you are forced to kill the *kaboko* in defense, later on someone will get sick. The dead ancestor spirits are the culprits. When this kind of situation occurs, you have to perform a cleansing ceremony at the *Mori Cana* to purify yourself."

Dead ancestors' spirits (*marapu*) can be vengeful, but they can also be benevolent. Pati Bebe describes this aspect of her Grandfather Python's personality as well. "The snake provides medicine to protect us from sickness, and to heal us."

While the Marapu Priests are the experts who are able to communicate with the ancestors during rituals, laypersons are able to communicate with their ancestors in dreams or in other special situations, such as during encounters in sacred forests.

Pati Bebe talks about communicating with her python ancestor in dreams: "If a snake bites you in a dream, he is giving you medicine because you are sick. If the snake does not bite you in your dream, then the ancestor is cleansing you . . . a spirit is at work. If you dream about a snake, we believe the ancestor will bring wealth to you in the form of water buffalo, horses, pigs, or cash. The ancestor-snake will deliver you out of poverty and bring you into safety."

More than one patriclan traces their ancestry to Grandfather Python: Umbu Ŋgedo is the name of the Wei Yeŋgho patriclan's Grandfather Python, Pala Kawata is the name of the Grandfather Python of the Bukubani patriclan, and Umbu Bobo is the Grandfather Python of patriclans in Karendi. Each of these patriclans say that their Grandfather Python was an original inhabitant of Kodi, a first "human" in the region, echoing the founder ideology commonly heard in Austronesian societies (Bellwood 2006). The story of Grandfather Python Umbu Ŋgedo is that he was one of four brothers who were the first Kodi people on Earth. These four brothers are the progenitors of all Kodi people, according to Marapu elder Kandi Homba who lives in Watu Katombo Hamlet, a satellite hamlet of Tossi Village settled by members of the clan Wei Yeŋgho. The brothers were Rato Pokil, Rato Mangil, Tukil Polo Kodi, and Kodi Umbu Ŋgedo. Rato Pokil and Rato Mangil lived in the seaside village of Tossi.[2] These two brothers generated very large patriclans whose members continue to rally together in Tossi, their Great Clan Village, for the annual seaworm and pasola ceremonies. Rato Pokil and Rato Mangil gave to Tukil Polo Kodi the land for the Great Clan Village Mabaha, which continues to be the center of power in the Kodi Bokolo region, and the sacred forest Deha. Rato Pokil and Rato Mangil gave to Kodi Umbu Ŋgedo the land for the Great Clan Village Wei Yeŋgho, which is the center of power in the Kodi Bangedo region, and the sacred forest Kaniŋyo. The four brothers' story is an Austronesian narrative about social organization, social rank, and territory.

Umbu Ŋgedo from Wei Yeŋgho, known as Grandfather Python, was a transspecies character. Originally a python, he transformed into a human when he fell in love with a human woman, married her, and became the father of human children. When Petrus, a descendant of Grandfather Python, talks about pythons, he uses the Indonesian word "*orang*," which is the same word he uses to refer to the human taxa.

Petrus, who lives in Pemukiman Hamlet, says, "If a person kills a python, he has to sacrifice a pig [this is a euphemism for hosting a *yaigho* ceremony] so that the soul of the python will come back down to Earth from the Moon Sun. If he does not sacrifice a pig, he will become sick. The person becomes sick because the soul of the snake wraps itself around the murderer's middle section and stops up his intestines. The angry, displaced soul of the pyt' ɔn makes it so that the murderer cannot eat for so long that he becom ɔo skinny and dies."

When a soul is displaced, all of the universe's beings are involved with getting it back to the right place. When one person, animal, or plant is sick, all beings come together (some reluctantly, some willingly) for the healing. Profound interdependencies exist among the universe's many nonhuman subjects, living Kodi people, and dead Kodi persons whose spirits are still active on Earth and beyond Earth. The lives of Earthbound beings and celestial bodies literally revolve around one another since the Moon is the satellite of the Earth and the Earth-Moon system is the satellite of the Sun.

HEALING SOCIAL RELATIONSHIPS

Yaigho serve multiple agendas for the priest-performers, hosts, and attendees. *Yaigho* simultaneously serve to retrieve displaced souls, to heal inflicted living humans, plants, and animals, and to repair relationships between living humans and all other beings—living and nonliving, human and nonhuman. During *yaigho*, the attendees communicate with the living and nonliving, human and nonhuman. *Yaigho* rituals figuratively "heal" relationships between the living and the dead, and they also physically "heal" the living as we see in Hona Tiela's and Petrus's descriptions of the consequences of neglecting *toyo yaigho*.

The lead healers, soul retrievers, and performers in a *yaigho* ceremony are the chanter, drummer, gong players, and the diviner (Hoskins 1996). The chanters, or *toyo yaigho*, are fluent in a special linguistic register Marapu elders speak during ritual occasions. Members of the community who are not rituals officials are not fluent in this linguistic register. The ritual register includes special terminology referencing the spiritual world and recalling historical figures and events. The ritual register has a couplet structure consisting of a paired line followed by a grammatical stop. The couplets are metered, so chanters recite them rhythmically. An example is the following list of tools the *yaigho* performers put inside their drums. These are the necessary tools for retrieving souls from the Moon Sun.

Kandiri kuta ligha Kabindi wini toro	Betel leaves Areca nuts
Karanda kenda bendu Kambola ughe longhe	Wooden drum Wild yam twine
Talu tongol wu lughale Pitu lighit wu kawalu	Three wild yam tubers Four candlenuts
Ⅰ ˑdo mata Lod'do Pana mata 'la	Bow to the Sun's eye Arrow to the Moon's eye

The Marapu Priest Hona Tiela says that he and his fellow priests, "use chanting and drumming to shoot an arrow toward the Moon Sun when we need to bring a soul back to Earth. The drum needs a bow and arrow to shoot up to the *Witi Wulla Limya Lod'do* (Foot of the Moon Hand of the Sun). When the priests are successful, the arrow spears the displaced soul, and pulls it back down to Earth."

Hona Tiela's explanation reveals how the drum is also an actor and an active companion in the priests' pursuits. While the drummer plays the drum and the *toyo yaigho* chants couplets, the rhythm is as distinct from everyday speech as when poets recite poetry. The ritual terminology is also distinct. The three-word term *kandiri kuta ligha* identifies betel leaves in ritual performances, *ro utta* is the common everyday term for betel leaves. When ritual performers refer to areca nuts as *kabindi wini toro* in *yaigho* rituals, commoners call them *lab'ba* in everyday conversations. The ritual terminology is taboo in nonritual situations. The betel leaves and areca nuts themselves resolve the taboo-ness of their ritual names when, at the beginning of *yaigho* ceremonies, Marapu elders place areca and betel inside the *tambur* (drum) body as an offering to the drum so that it will speak fluently once the chanter begins chanting. The betel and areca have agency, as do the other botanical tools of yams and candlenuts.

One ritual drummer said that these botanical tools, "help the drum organize the taboo sentences so that the *rato* (priest, elder, healer) can talk for a long, long time without his words being taboo."

Betel and areca appear in many Marapu rituals, including *yaigho* (soul retrieval, healing), *wolek* (feast honoring the ancestors), *parupu kaloro* (divination), *nale* (seaworm), and *pasola* (horse jousting) ceremonies. Pieces of areca nuts and betel leaves are also presented to the ancestor spirits on any occasions when elders recite clan histories and when offerings are placed on ancestors' graves. Betel and areca are the offerings of choice for ritual performers because the ancestors who receive the offerings prefer these cordials over all others. Making offerings of betel and areca nullify taboos on certain types of speech, including the ritual couplets mentioned above and also the oral histories "owned" by elders that recount the exploits of the ancestors and recite the traditional names of the sacred places where the ancestors' exploits occurred, or their "footprints" (Fowler 2003).

CELESTIAL BODIES AS COMPANIONS FOR HUMAN BODIES IN A BIOSOCIAL UNIVERSE

This chapter and the preceding one have taken culturally significant, nonliving, non-Earthbound resources and shown how even nonliving, nonearthly beings are members of the same biosocial worlds that living, Earthbound taxa inhabit. In this chapter and chapter 4, I have extended the purview of social theory to encompass abiotics as well as extraterrestrials by describing the ways biotic bodies relate to celestial bodies.

Kodi perceive celestial bodies to be their active companions in an expansive biosocial world, in an expanding universe. Kodi know the sky's inhabitants from an Earthbound perspective, and they believe the sky's inhabitants have an extraterrestrial perspective. Extraterrestrial actants have their own agendas and methods for pursuing them that are knowable from within the context of Kodi cosmology. As subjective selves, the sky's actants are both the ones observed and ones observing, and they are both the ones produced and the ones producing. Kodi devote much effort to maintaining "right" relations with celestial bodies because they see themselves as co-producing this biosocial world with them. People weave their personal and cultural identities together with the Moon Sun. The personal and collective Kodi identities are not only mutually created but also continuously reconstituted in relation to the Moon Sun.

Chapters 4 and 5 have brought us closer to recognizing how profoundly Earth's living beings are affected by nonliving, non-Earthlings by pointing to specific Indigenous understandings of celestial bodies and then adding on scientific information about those same astronomical objects. Scientific astronomy is useful here in anthropological translations of Indigenous people's knowledges about the universe as a method for seeing into the Other's perspective. The Other in this case is not only Kodi persons, but also nonhuman, nonliving, and non-Earthly beings. Collectively, the theoretical innovations in multispecies ethnography, biocultural becomings, posthumanism, agential realism, and new materialism beg researchers to try to figure out the many ways humans are entangled with nonhumans. One method for figuring this out is to adopt the perspectives of nonhumans.

In chapters 4 and 5, I have described in-depth an Indigenous community's perspective wherein people attempt to access extraterrestrial perspectives. In this case, the ethnographic *field* became the *sky* as, when I asked my Kodi colleagues to tell me about themselves, they directed my attention upward into the blue atmosphere, and as local Marapu specialists interviewed Earth's orbital companions about their *selves* during rituals and prayers. I have also brought in the comparative case of astronomers who are a group of scientists whose *field* (i.e., the geographic source of data) is the *sky*. This shifting perspective renders the *sky* as a "vast relational field" (Skafish 2014: 24) as well as a deep translational *field*.

Juxtaposing sky and field reveals similarities and differences in the ways Kodi non-scientists and non-Kodi scientists construct extraterrestrial actants and their relationships with humans. Kodi and scientists enthusiastically seek knowledge about the sky and its inhabitants. Members of both communities express strong desires to connect with the universe's objects. The intent to know and connect seems necessary for the wellbeing of scientists when they feel are intellectually "hungry" and the Kodi when they are inspired to perform *yaigho*. Engaging in relationships with celestial bodies expresses important values and fulfills critical needs to connect, know, and heal.

NOTES

1. Lidia recited these first two lines in the Indonesian national language. She uses the Kodi language to recite the other lines in her prayer.

2. To visualize the location of Tossi, refer to "Map 3. The Location of Traditional Territories (*Kabihu*) and Ancestral Villages in Kodi" on page 7 in Hoskins (1993).

Chapter 6

Sequential Synchronies in Multispecies Interactions and Biosocial Change

SYNCHRONIES IN SEQUENCES

Sequential synchronies explain vital dimensions of change in the biosocial worlds of Kodi. Humans recognize sequential synchronies in nature, and find them to be especially rich symbolic schemes. A sequential synchrony is a regularly repeating phenomena during which a montage of entities coordinate their activities with one another so that they form a biosocial collective. The entities who participate in the sequential synchrony have at least one activity or process that co-occurs in at least one biosocially significant instance with the activities or processes of the other entities in their collectives. The activities or processes that entities contribute to the sequential synchronic phenomena may be chemical, biological, social, geophysical, spiritual, or of some other type. The entities and assemblages who participate in sequential synchronies define temporal intervals and spatial extents as they coordinate themselves into co-occurring phenomena. Sequential synchronies thus construct not only space-time but they also construct biosocial worlds.

Sequential synchronies explain the relationships between Kodi people and Sumba's dynamic seascapes and landscapes to be causal, or meaningful, or both. People recognize their own experiences with living and dying when they witness the lives, development, and deaths of living, Earthbound bodies and even nonliving celestial bodies. When Kodi people recognize similarities in the behaviors of constituents of their environments, they associate them with one another and give meaning to the associations. Meanings emerge in the form of sequential synchronies: the living records of repeating, serial space-time correspondences in the behaviors of environmental actors and the occurrences of events. In some instances, meaning is what constitutes the simultaneous interactions between actors (Tarnas 2006).

In some cases, meaning, rather than causality (Tarnas 2006), is the glue that holds actors or events together into groups of associated entities. An example is the correspondence between *kadere nale*, the ritualized gathering of polychaetes by Kodi people, and the swarming of polychaetes in the reefs along Kodi's shores. In other cases, the activities among actors are causal, or at least partly causal. The Moon's altitude relative to the Sun's causes polychaete spawning via shifts from bluish sunlight to reddish moonlight. Additional mechanisms, both internal and external to polychaetes, co-occur with the Sunlight-Moonlight correspondences. That some correspondences are meaningful and not necessarily causal, and others are both causal and meaningful argues for a multidisciplinary methodology that involves, in the case of the Sun-Moon-polychaete-human synchrony, referencing the findings of astronomy, marine biology, and ethnography.

Sequential synchronies are one among many forms that change takes, but one that is especially stimulating for humans. Through cultural representations, human communities account for patterned changes in space-time that are sequential synchronies. Humans recognize sequential synchronies from the myriad viewpoints we occupy ranging from ground-level Earth from where we can look around our own planet and up into the sky, to the Moon's surface from where we (or, at least those of us with access to imagery from space) can see the Blue Marble in a new light, to the orbital spheres where satellite sensors capture the Earth's changing surface. Human methods for detecting sequential synchronies range widely as well: from our bodies' own sensing faculties to the high-tech, ground-based, and space-based equipment that can detect the activities of distant objects and phenomena. Whatever faculties or gear we use to observe the universe, and from whatever physical place we observe it, we interpret the universe within intersubjective communities consisting of a cacophony of stimuli contributed by human, nonhuman, Earthly, extraterrestrial, visible, and invisible bodies.

The occurrence of sequential synchronies is an independent reality, verified by multiple epistemologies, ranging from the scientific to the Indigenous, and spanning long temporal intervals and spatial extents. People engage with sequential synchronies through diverse modes of being that influence what the independent reality indexes for them. Human communities interpret the sequential synchronies sometimes in terms of the values they wish to emphasize, the aspects of their identities they wish to highlight, the politics they wish to promote, the experiences they wish to remember, or in some other terms. Some people in some situations might use sequential synchronies to express values related to their clan memberships or their professional affiliations, their desires for love or their desires for data, their need to eat or their need to publish, their will to survive or their drive to discover, or some other values.

The entities involved in the sequential synchronies are involved in distinctly patterned changing space-time at multiple levels: at the biosocial community level as contributors to sequential synchronies and also at the single taxa level as agents of change. These entities' involvement in sequential synchronies is not the only way for us to view how they contribute to our changing universe. Space-time involvements are discernable at multiple levels from the individual level to the biosocial group level (Wassman and Dasen 2000). If we consider the universe to be an individual actant, we see that it pulls the Sun, Moon, Earth, and rest of our Solar System and everything surrounding it toward its horizon. Taking the Moon as another example, its participation in change looks different depending upon the scale at which we view it. At the single taxa level, the Moon belongs in the category of "satellites" that includes the two sub-categories of natural satellites and artificial satellites. "Natural satellite" is a clade of objects that orbit larger objects, including planets and asteroids. Within our Solar System, moons are natural satellites of planets, known as their primaries. In addition to Earth's Moon, other examples of natural satellites are Titan, Enceladus, and Saturn's many other moons; Ganymede and Jupiter's other moons; Phobos and Deimos orbiting Mars; Triton orbiting Neptune; and Uranus's moons. Artificial satellites are the manned and robotic spacecrafts that orbit astronomical objects, such as the instruments orbiting the Earth, Venus, Saturn, Jupiter, Mars, and Eros. The sensors aboard the artificial satellites LANDSAT, MODIS, TERRA, and AQUA create the images that scientists use to study critical environmental changes related to weather, climate, and human activities. Our Solar System's planets and their satellites form "satellite systems" that orbit the Sun as units bound together by gravity. The Earth-Moon system is an example of a satellite system that orbits the common center of gravity that is the Sun.

In our Earth-Moon system, the satellite and its primary have synchronous orbits which are evident to us in the fact that us Earthlings always and only see one side of the Moon. The Moon rotates on its own axis in the same amount of time as it traverses its orbit around the Earth. The Moon has a synchronous rotation because its rotation is equal to its revolution. The lunar day and the lunar year are twenty-seven days, equal to an Earth month. All Earthlings experience this same time interval, no matter our geographical location or socioeconomic status. How we interpret the Earth-Moon relationship—whether or not we even notice their orbits and their synchrony—does vary depending on our positionality and subjectivity. Thus, in addition to viewing the Moon at the taxonomic levels of satellite system, satellite, and natural satellite, we also gain much insight by considering its role in change at the individual level. The Moon is a singular object as the Earth's only natural satellite, second to the Sun as the brightest object in Earth's sky, and the largest natural satellite in the universe relative to its primary. Moreover, the Moon is one member of a biosocial collective, as well as a member of all Earthlings' biosocial collectives.

Delving into the Earth-Moon system with the idea of synchrony in mind, we find more simultaneous phenomena are happening than just the two astronomical bodies' orbits. The argument could be made that all phenomena happening at any given moment in the universe are synchronous. The list of potential examples may be infinite. But that might be overstating things, and it would diminish the extraordinary synchronous scheme that is defined by the content of this book. The list of synchronous phenomena that happen sequentially and that are periodically repeated is much shorter, but still a long one. Out of all of the potential examples, this book highlights the one simple yet vivid, ethnographically grounded yet theoretically informative sequential synchrony involving lunar periodicity, polychaete spawning, and rice ripening. Kodi communities translate and transfer the annual correspondence between the Moon's waning, polychaete swarming, and rice reproduction into traditional calendar (see Table 2.1). The series of three seaworm months together symbolize the synchrony between the Moon, polychaetes, and rice. Kodi people insert their own iconic behaviors into the synchrony by designating the space-time of the polychaete swarms and the rice harvests as the same space-time for the most important rituals in the annual cycle. The fact that the seaworm rituals occur as a series of ceremonies whose times, spaces, and performances relative to one another are rule-based and coordinate the activities of a large group of people further indexes the sequential and synchronic character of environmental patterns.

The relationship between the Moon, polychaetes, rice, and people is synchronous because it is coordinated in space-time, and it is sequential because it happens during every annual cycle. The series of three seaworm months initiates the beginning of each annual cycle, and is the first in a series of sequences that precedes an annually-repeated series of other synchronies. Following the seaworm synchrony, additional temporally and spatially coordinated behaviors occur between various entities and are cited in the names of months. The month names are the key symbols of the synchronies, which in order are: flowering trees, ritual feasting, more flowering trees, ritual quietude, bird nesting, and mushroom sprouting (see Table 2.1). In this serial collection of symbols of synchronies, humans and nonhumans alternate as key symbols of transspecies correspondences. Kodi's traditional calendar is a culturally-specific articulation of what people sense and perceive, and what they experience and know in their own local environments. In their traditional calendar, Kodi express the great value they give to coordinating their own human-like activities with the patterns and processes of other biotic and abiotic entities. The calendrical artifact of Kodi space-time indexes the biosocial relationships specific to this community.

Based on his ethnographic research in Indonesia Orr has found that, "the same environmental stimuli can be perceived differently, reflecting variance in both perceptual skills and interpretive techniques" (Orr 2016: 68). This may be true at the level of some of the constituents of sequential synchronies. So, for example, people across cultures may vary in how they perceive and interpret the swarming of marine species. At the broader level of multispecies coordinations similar variations may still occur. Yet, interestingly, people from a diversity of cultures similarly perceive the periodically repeating coordinations of multiple entities and interpret them into cultural systems for organizing themselves spatially and temporally. These space-time cultures do vary, of course, in the form, for example, of variations in traditional ritual calendars. But even traditional ritual calendars in many Austronesian and Papuan communities share the characteristics of having designs reflecting special multispecies coordinations and of guiding people to coordinate their subsistence and spiritual activities with the other entities' coordinations. Many of the entities who are involved in the repeating, coordinated activities vary from ecosystem to ecosystem. Some of the same entities are involved regardless of the ecosystem; namely, the Earth, Moon, and Sun. Though, even with the Earth, Moon, and Sun, the details about their spatial and temporal aspects varies geographically and over time. In the case of polychaetes, people living in widely dispersed communities recognize the lunar periodicity of their breeding behavior, but variations exist between the communities in the species of polychaetes and the annual periodicity of the coordination of their swarming with the Moon.

The perception and interpretation of the environmental stimuli of sequential synchronies is widespread, but the ways for sensing stimuli, the epistemologies of knowing, and the content of the interpretations vary. Sumbanese biosocial collectives are unique, but the symbolic and linguistic lives of contemporary Sumbanese connect to the lives of people living in communities throughout Eastern Indonesia as well as across the Austronesian and Papuan domains. The coordination of polychaete breeding with lunar periodicity and with human activities is a very special type of environmental stimuli that people throughout Indo-Pacific region sense, perceive, interpret, know, and act in response to.

ECOSYSTEM ENGINEERS WORKING TOGETHER TO BUILD BIOSOCIAL NETWORKS

The term "biosocial network" as I use it here in *Biosocial Synchrony on Sumba* builds on the concept of "biosocial" in the edited volume *Biosocial Becomings* (Ingold and Palsson 2013) and also on the concept of "ecological networks" in *Ecology, The Ascendant Perspective* (Ulanowicz 1997) and subsequent publications on ecological networks. Ecological networks are contingent collections of abiotic and biotic entities who connect through their interactions and through coupled processes (Wright and Jones 2006). Ecological networks configure themselves via the organizational forces of competition, mutualism, feedbacks, cascades, limiting factors, dynamics, regime shifts, emergence, chaos, disturbance, migration, and flows of matter, energy, and information. The connections that bind species in ecological networks are based on conditional principles of adaptation, evolution, and coevolution. Ecological networks are complex adaptive systems (Ulanowicz 1997) where "lots of things are put together in the same place" (Ulanowicz 1997), and where these "things" respond to one another, at varying temporal scales, genetically and phenotypically. Contingency and conditionality of the species interactions in ecological networks are due to "local and historical circumstances and interfering events" (Olff et al. 2009, under "Ecological Interaction Webs as Complex Adaptive Systems").

Members of biosocial networks engage in spatial and temporal interactions, and evolve together as geographic mosaics (Olff et al. 2009; Thompson 2005). The human-polychaete-Earth-Moon-Sun nexus is the sub-network in Kodi's biosocial network that is the subject of this book. The main types of interactions[1] involving humans, landscapes, polychaetes, and celestial bodies that are described in *Biosocial Synchrony on Sumba* are: (i) space-time involvements, (ii) multispecies correspondences, (iii) synchronous behaviors among species within networks, (iv) interactions among human individuals' socioculturally conditioned senses, experiences, and perceptions, (v) consumer-resource and signifier-sign interactions, (vi) biotic and abiotic interactions, (vii) interactions between symbolic or ritual objects and signifying humans or ritual performers, (viii) living beings and beings in the afterlife (ix) Earthbound beings and extraterrestrial entities, and (x) multispecies interactions in terrestrial and marine ecosystems.

The biotic components of Kodi's biosocial network who are the main subjects of *Biosocial Synchrony on Sumba* are (i) humans, (ii) plants, (iii) land animals, and (iv) marine organisms. The main abiotic components of Kodi's biosocial networks that are featured in this book are (i) abiotic resources (e.g., light), (ii) environmental conditions and processes (e.g., weather, climate, tide levels, celestial cycles, fire regimes, oscillations, monsoons, winds, ocean currents), (iii) nonliving entities (e.g., planets and celestial bodies [especially the Earth, Moon, Sun, and Venus]), (iv) dwelling and interacting sites (e.g., houses, hamlets, villages, ceremonial sites, beaches, coral reefs, ocean benthos), and (v) technologies (Kodi's ritual tools and astronomy's research tools).[2]

In this book, I have explored "how species coevolve across complex landscapes amid interactions with multiple other species" (Thompson 2005: 3) by describing how a select group of entities living within the Kodi biosociety work together to change Kodi's biosociety. Humans, polychaetes, the Moon, and Sun affect one another along several intersecting pathways, including the several that have been mentioned in this book: ecosystem engineering, synchrony, predator-prey or consumer-resource interactions (Wright and Jones 2006); population structure, increased or decreased biodiversity, relative proportions of native to invasive species (Crooks 2002); benthic and reef formations, biogeochemical alterations, hydrological flows, geological formations, erosion and sedimentation, soil structure and moisture, nutrient cycling (Zulkifly et al. 2013); and hormonal fluctuations, tidal fluctuations, and spectral dynamics. This list contains only the pathways mentioned in this book, and is not an exhaustive list of all of the forces at play in the actual biosocial network. The first two pathways of ecosystem engineering and synchrony are the ones that I have explored most closely in *Biosocial Synchrony on Sumba*.

HUMANS, POLYCHAETES, AND THE MOON AS ECOSYSTEM ENGINEERS

Humans, polychaetes, and the Moon are ecosystem engineers because they modify biophysical environments and they respond to others' modifications. The ways these components of Kodi's biosocial network engineer their ecosystems are numerous and complex. This brief section contains an inventory of the ecosystem engineering activities enacted by humans, polychaetes, and the Moon that are mentioned in this book.

In general, humans are ecosystem engineers (Bird 2015) who cause change by interacting with, modifying, moving, creating, and recreating material items. Humans enact change by accumulating, interpreting, and sharing immaterial items of culture. The people who live in Kodi create, modify, and maintain habitats by working with the ecological conditions of their island home and by enacting their space-time culture in their homelands. The following list identifies some instances of ecosystem engineering by Kodi people. Kodi people modify:

- myriad ecosystems through their interactions with plant, animal, and abiotic components of landscapes and seascapes
- landscapes and seascapes during the course of enacting ritual practices related to their customary calendar
- land-based ecosystems when engaging in activities related to horticulture, agriculture, arboriculture, animal husbandry, pastoralism, forestry, hunting, gathering, fishing, and other economic pursuits

- land cover through planting, pruning, weeding, harvesting, and otherwise manipulating cultivated, semi-cultivated, and wild plants
- nearshore and tidal reef habitats where polychaetes live while foraging for reef-dwelling species by walking through the reefs, by line-fishing from shore, and by fishing from boats

Polychaetes are ecosystem engineers who affect their abiotic and biotic habitats, and they are affected by other organisms' engineering of their ecosystems, including the other reef-building and benthos-building species; predator fish, shellfish, birds; humans; the Moon; the Sun; and other organisms and entities. Polychaetes modify their habitats through bioturbation, consumption, excretion, nutrient production, swarming, and in the following additional ways:

- members of the Sedentaria subgroup affect the physical substrate by burrowing and boring holes in the sea floor and in reefs
- tube-dwelling polychaetes modify their habitat by constructing tubes that, when concentrated in larger patches, build reefs (Rabaut, Vincx, and Degraer 2009)
- digging polychaetes cause bioturbation by reworking sediments and repositioning microorganisms
- polychaetes cause bioturbation by consuming and depositing detritus
- through bioturbation, some species increase the texture and aeration of sediments, the suspension of sediments and minerals, and water turbidity
- tube-dwelling species decrease sediment suspension by using mucus or slime to glue sediment and shell fragments together in making tubes
- benthic dwelling polychaetes consume detritus, algae, and microalgae
  - some species of algae are themselves engineers of some aquatic ecosystems (Zulkifly et al. 2013)
- benthic dwellers produce sediment and food—the detritus eaten by other microbivores and the mineralized nutrients eaten by microalgae
- habitat modification by polychaetes influences the abundance and distribution of other organisms in the benthic zones and on reefs (Feral 1989)
- swarming polychaetes attract predators to spawning sites
- swarming polychaetes attract human and bird consumers to tidal reefs where humans and wading birds walk on the reefs in the course of capturing prey and thereby impact the reefs as well as affect other interactions happening on the reefs
- polychaetes' ecosystem engineering behaviors lead to "interaction modification" (Arditi et al. 2005), or changes in ecosystems that affect the interactions other organisms have with their food resources

The Moon is an ecosystem engineer when it modifies the habitats where humans and polychaetes live, and it is in turn engineered by the modifying effects of the Earth as a whole. The Moon modifies Earthly habitats and is an ecosystem engineer because the Moon:

- shapes daily, monthly, and seasonal space-time
- engineers aspects of the marine environment via its effects on tides
- modifies spectral environments by affecting twilight chromaticity
- varies over daily, monthly, and annual cycles causing fluctuations in tides, twilight chromaticity, and other processes and phenomena

Humans and polychaetes respond both biologically—in ways related to reproduction, energy input or nutrition, and movement or energy exertion—and behaviorally, by altering their own habitat modification activities in response to each other's and the Moon's influences. Many other biotic and abiotic entities participate in biosocial change processes, but these are 'he ones I focus on here in this book. These biotic (humans and polychaete' .nd abiotic (the Moon) entities function as ecosystem engineers in Kodi's biosocial network, which is composed of a multitude of engineers.

COHERENTLY CONSTRUCTING BIOSOCIAL WORLDS

While the biosocial relationships that I describe in *Biosocial Synchrony on Sumba* are contemporary ones, they are also ones that have persisted for a very long time. The history of the origins and migrations of Austronesians partly explain the cross-cultural persistence and continuing existence of specific traits, which are part of the biosocial relationships that have been highlighted in this ethnography. That the relationships between people and plants, animals, and celestial bodies are both ancient and ongoing is evident in the numerous aspects of Kodi culture that are also found among other Southeast Asian (such as the cross-cultural similarities discussed in Tannenbaum and Kammerer 2003), Austronesian (as detailed in Bellwood, Fox, and Tryon 2006), and integrated Austronesian-Papuan societies. Among the traits found cross-culturally in these regions, is that communities' traditional annual calendars symbolize sequential synchronies and combine environmental patterns with ritual routines. Many Southeast Asian, Austronesian, and Austronesian-Papuan communities reference especially spectacular ecological sequences and synchronies in the design of their space-time cultures. People manipulate their surroundings based on who they understand themselves and their companions to be.

The collection of entities with whom humans live varies spatially and temporally due to ecological variations and changing conditions. Yet, the communities who have lived in the Indo-Pacific region have lived close to polychaete swarms for many generations, have harvested important plants at approximately the same time as the polychaetes swarm, and have brought their own practices into sync with the overlaps between polychaete spawnings, harvests, and the waning Moon. These correspondences may have been going on long enough to constitute some degree of coevolution. The possibility that humans, seaworms, the Moon, and island landscapes have coevolved is more likely if we accept the validity of niche construction theory (Odling-Smee, Laland, and Feldman 2013). The application of niche construction theory to the sequential synchronies on Indo-Pacific islands would posit the Moon, the Sun, humans, and Annelids (the phylum that includes polychaetes, earthworms, and leaches) as ecological engineers who have modified their surroundings and thereby intervened in their own evolution and the evolut⁀ ˑ of the other beings who inhabit those same ecosystems (Laland 2013). I   ˑ's environmental experiences develop together with the entities who co-i.....abit their shared ecological inheritances (Odling-Smee, Laland, and Feldman 2013).

Niche construction theory is an intelligent revision of Darwinian evolution, and it has convenient points of convergence with other brilliant endeavors to improve evolutionary theories, it could be more inclusive of the myriad change agents if it were to include nonliving entities side-by-side with living organisms. Niche construction theory has a bias for life as illustrated by the focus on living organisms here in a statement from Laland's explication of niche construction theory: "From the beginning of life, all organisms have always, in part, modified their selective environments by niche construction, and their ability to do so has always, in part, been a consequence of natural selection" (Laland 2013: 433). The same is true for Ingold's biosocial evolution as well as Kirksey, Hartigan, Tsing et al.'s multispecies ethnography. Supporting this argument if we come to it with an Earth-centric perspective is more difficult than if we approach it from the perspective of an expanding universe. At the planetary scale, many of us can look at rocks, for example, through our cultural lenses and feel confident that they are not living organisms. At the universal scale, we can look through astronomers' lenses to see that flows of space-time, matter, energy, and forces such as gravity and thermonuclear reactions co-construct our bodies in ways that affect how we co-construct our niches.

The universe in its possibly infinite boundlessness embodies its own ecological inheritances. Continuous change is an inherited trait of our expanding universe. Pinpointing the beginning of change or identifying some time before which the universe was not changing is difficult. The Big Bang birthed our universe 10–20 billion years ago, but it could not give birth to change if it is itself an outcome of change. The universe as a whole is heading somewhere fast and, while some astronomers speculate where it might be going, they have difficulty predicting the endpoint of change.

On the much, much smaller scale, determining what the conditions were like on Sumba Island prior to the time when the island began changing is also challenging. Yet, identifying temporal ranges for the rebooting of the island's ecology is not as tremendous of a task as attempting to do that for the entire universe would be. The island's biotic-abiotic assemblages are "temporary collections" (a phrase Durham [2002: 193] uses to define cultures) of "abiotic, biotic, and social components (and their interactions)" (Hobbs et al. 2013: 58).

The biosocial evolution of Sumba has been punctuated by the crossing of thresholds when combinations of geological, climatological, ecological, and social processes reset space-time and cleared the way for the emergence of new ecosystems. Periodically during the island's history, new ecosystems have emerged when the composition of biotic-abiotic assemblages shifted enough that the functions of ecological communities changed enough that they crossed thresholds and turned into categorically different types of communities. In some instances, the island as a whole crossed thresholds, while in other cases single communities or collections of communities crossed thresholds. Human agency has not been involved in the emergence of all novel ecosystems on Sumba. Prior to the arrival of the first human settlers on the island, geology, climate, and biological colonization were major drivers of ecological turnover.

Sumba Island has experienced successive categorical ecological reconfigurations in its 420 million-year-long existence. Sumba was originally part of the Australian and/or Asian continents. Tectonic activities caused the island to break away from the Australian or Asian continent and move around the region. Long-term climate changes caused the island to be completely inundated by seawater when the global climate warmed, glaciers melted, and sea levels rose, and to later reemerge above sea level when the climate cooled, glaciers grew, and sea levels dropped. The oceans surrounding Sumba have been defining forces throughout the island's social and ecological history. Even now, the Indian Ocean on the island's southern border, the Savu Sea on the northeastern coast, and the Sumba Strait on the northwestern coast shape the island's reefs and beaches.

When Sumba Island was completely underwater, prior vegetative communities would presumably have died off. When the island re-emerged above sea level, new plant species would have colonized the fresh land and assembled themselves into ephemeral communities whose legacies are today's changing vegetative communities. Against a dramatically changing background, evidence for the long-term existence of at least two types of ecosystems, savannas and lowland monsoon forests, comes from looking to the island's endemic bird, butterfly, plant, and animal species. The island has many endemic species dispersed among the savannas and forests that are presumably long-existing ecological communities on the island. At least two endemic species—the sundew plant (*Drosera indica* L. Droseraceae) and the Sumba buttonquail (*Turnix everetti* Hartert Turnicidae)—are adapted to savannas. These endemic species would have evolved within Sumba's savannas, a process that would require the long-term presence of savannas on the island.

Evidence of the long-term presence of lowland monsoon forests comes from the fact that they host populations of endemic butterflies. Those lowland monsoon forests that are protected primary forests have higher densities of endemic butterfly species that are specialized feeders on plant species that are also found in those forests. Unprotected secondary forests have lower densities of endemic species, and higher densities of butterfly species that have wide geographic ranges and are generalized feeders on host plants. Unprotected secondary lowland monsoon forests have higher diversities of butterfly species as well. Greater variation in forest structure and more microhabitats, in addition to butterfly adaptations to generalized feeding, partly explain the higher butterfly diversity. The higher butterfly diversity in secondary disturbed forests indicates that "human disturbance" (Hamer et al. 1997: 72, though they provide no details about human activities) increases total species diversity while it decreases endemic diversity (Hamer et al. 1997). The transition from climax forests to secondary scrub, creates new habitats for "migratory habitat generalists that can rapidly invade disturbed forest habitats" (Hamer et al. 1997: 21). Hamer et al. favor the unconverted, primary forest for protection of endemic species and the conservation of global biodiversity. In this example, biosocial evolutionary theory presents the possibility for judging some anthropogenic changes in ecosystem composition, structure, and function as being beneficial for biodiversity but detrimental for endemism.

The ecological engineering of Sumba by humans may date back as far as 14,000 years. But the archaeology is so incomplete that this is only a placeholder date until more information is available about the island's history. The arrival of humans would have initiated the beginning of the kind of biosocial evolution that would have included humans as the social animal with the dominant role in the construction of Sumbanese worlds. The first Austronesian horticulturalists arrived on Sumba around 4875 BP (Lansing et al. 2007). Austronesian horticultural activities, such as forest clearing, burning and the introduction of new species, would have pressed ecological communities toward novel types. The island's human communities have served as partners with ecology in the construction of savannas, forests, and particular types of niches that are favorable for humans. As ecological engineers, past peoples sculpted the landscapes that are the ecological inheritances of today's people. Moreover, changes in human migration, subsistence regimes, and political economies co-evolve with dynamic tectonic, climatological, and oceanographic processes.

THEORETICAL IMPLICATIONS OF THE KODI COSMOVISION

In what ways does this study contribute to theories about the evolution of humans, nonhuman organisms, and the universe more broadly? The cosmology of the Indigenous Kodi collective has the potential to enlighten the environmental sciences and social theory. The Kodi cosmos is a biosocial one where space-time dynamics involve interactions among and correspondences between multiple species, living and nonliving entities, Earthly and Universal subjects, visible and invisible actors. These agents are all entangled in fluid fields and coevolve in space-time continuums. Kodi epistemologies provide access to these biosocial worlds through culturally specific but also cross-culturally patterned methods of sensing, classifying, and interpreting. Where I have already in the preceding chapters encouraged opening multispecies ethnography to nonliving identities, now I want to add opening biosocial theory up to being a counter-cosmology, and not just a social theory. This book as a whole presents one particular and especially intriguing biosocial counter-cosmology.

In the Kodi cosmovision, agents of many types enact change. Among the change agents are living people because Kodi conceptualize much change as anthropogenic. Nonliving humans also cause changes; in fact, Kodi point to the spirits as causing many of the changes in the weather and climate, in geophysical formations, and in the health of people, plants, and animals. Changes that occur in visible realms affect the invisible realm. An example is that when bodies die in the visible world, the invisible world gains more souls. Another example is that when ancestor spirits in the invisible realms respond emotionally and biophysically to human mental conditions and physical activities in the visible realm. Kodi conceptualize temporal change as co-occurring with spatial change, but the ways these are coupled varies. Some changes are reversible, including the return to Earth of souls who escaped to the Moon Sun. Other changes are irreversible, such as the walkabout journeys when the ancient ancestors left their footprints and journeys of souls into the afterlife.

Kodi believe that past peoples caused things to be the way they are now and they still have agency in the world. The agency of the ancestors is visible in the lightning, rain, Moon, Sun, and in their souls' other embodiments. The first group of humans to shape the island's biogeography were autochthons whose origins were in the python-human, lobster-human, crocodile-human, rat-human, goat-human, and other transtaxa beings. The second group began impacting the island environment after they arrived on the island by boat, as recounted in the footprint genre of stories. The autochthons were hunter gatherers who interacted with the island's given flora and fauna. The later-arrivals invented horticulture, and began clearing the land to plant crops, as recounted in the Biri Koni myth. The first horticulturalists and subsequent land-clearers and their descendants have been clearing the primary forests since then to the point where, according to Guru Ben, "There are no primary forests (Indonesian *hutan*) in Kodi or on Sumba anymore. Only secondary scrub forests (Indonesian *belukar toka*) are left on this island, and these are not the same as the primary forests."

Guru Ben expresses the opinion that some forests are "natural" and that the construction of some forests requires human agency, including the secondary scrub forests as well as the agroforests (*hemba*) that surround every Kodi settlement. Guru Ben makes some negative judgments about the loss of primary forests. Logging is charged with politics in Kodi today. When storytellers talk about the ancestors' resource management practices, however, they tend to venerate the ancestors for their good deeds relative to the landscape. Telling stories about the first immigrants to the island, the first migrants into territories occupied by the autochthons, the origins of seaworms, the origins of horticulture, the founders of hamlets who planted *Mori Cana*, and additional ritual speeches, are methods for negotiating the storytellers' status. When (mostly) men recite oral histories using ritual speech, they are doing the identity work they feel they need to do to raise or ensure their status. These stories about Sumbanese histories with undercurrents of spatial and temporal change, privilege the identities of some patrilineal descent groups relative to others.

The high-ranking patriarchs of patriclans perform their oral histories to serve their own agendas in their own times, and their politicking includes their claims to have inherited ownership rights to the ritual scripts from their fathers, uncles, and grandfathers. Assuming the scripts and/or their themes are at least partially consistent over time, the stories document biosocial changes that have taken place over multiple generations. In addition to the information contained in oral histories, Kodi accumulate information about biosocial changes through their own experiences. They personally witness biosocial changes over the course of their own lives. Most of their waking hours are spent outdoors, fully exposed to the environmental stimuli that they directly sense from a dwelling perspective.

Scientists, in comparison, remotely sense the Kodi environment from an aerial or extraterrestrial perspective. Scientists purportedly know change empirically, but in contrast to the personally-sensed experiences of Kodi agropastoralists, scientific empiricism has a different meaning. The empiricism of scientists' remotely-sensed experiences is mediated by nonhuman machines. Scientists rely on array of artificial agents to sense environments and turn their experiences into quantitative and visual data that scientists subsequently translate into knowledge about environmental change, and sometimes also propositions about the human agency involved in the change. When scientists claim that empiricism premises their epistemologies, they actually do not mean always first hand, in situ observation. They, in fact, sometimes doubt the validity of knowledge gained empirically, particularly when the first hand observers are local people who dwell in subject locations and who are not scientifically credentialed. Some scientists with this and similar biases sometimes rank their own epistemologies above dwelling methodologies for recording land use/land cover change, species' population changes (e.g., in butterflies, polychaetes, humans), ecosystem changes (e.g., forests transitioning to savannas), and dynamic fire regimes. Scientists privilege artificial intelligence over local intelligence for accurately identifying the short term change agents as weather and humans and the evolutionary change agents as inheritance, genetic drift, gene flow, mutation, natural ʿc-tion, and coevolution. In discussing how to factually understand environmental change, scientists put boundaries around local knowledge, juxtapose it to their more systematic knowledge, and define their own identities relative to others' identities.

Ecological knowledge and the experiences and epistemologies used to construct it as well as the identities built around it are relational. Comparing the ecological knowledge, experiences, epistemologies, and identities of the seemingly disparate communities of agropastoralists in the rural Global South with scientists in the urban Global North is a productive strategy because they do not exist in a vacuum. Different subjects come to know themselves and their worlds in different ways, and their ways of knowing and making worlds influences how they know and make themselves. Geophysicists, marine biologists, and astronomers stake their professional identities on being highly educated, technologically sophisticated, objective observers, meticulous data collectors, and emotionally-distant analyzers of a disenchanted world. Kodi people delineate their identities as being beholden to kin, obliged to participate in traditional exchanges, wary of the many risks to their survival, and devoted to staying in good stead with the personalities governing favorable or unfavorable conditions in an enchanted world.

In this admittedly oversimplified way of comparing how scientists and how Kodi project their identities, the Kodi identities are clearly relational, but the relational aspects of scientists' identities are not as obvious. This may be because one of the barriers to comparing the identities of scientists and Kodi is that scientists, like many Westerners, segregate their professional from their personal lives and the identity work they do is different for the different parts of their selves. Kodi do not distinguish between their lives at work and their lives outside of work in the same way, so their identities are more seamless across the various settings for their lives. Scientists' identities, even while performing their professional roles, are also relational even though this aspect of their identities may be masked in a scientific epistemological rhetoric.

Scientists, like Kodi, recognize that they live in the same space-time as the objects of their fascination; which are celestial bodies for astronomers, marine organisms for marine biologists, and the Earth's surface for geospatial analysts. Scientists and Kodi alike express the need to know their objects/subjects, and many also express the values of respect, care, attachment, and well wishes for their objects/subjects. Both types of people in this comparison desire to communicate and interact with nonhumans. They all, by one definition or another, see both humans and nonhumans as evolving; that is, as changing according to particular causes, effects, and mechanisms. All of the people in these comparisons engage in relationships with nonhumans. Giving r   ning to environmental experiences constitutes relating to other members c   's biosocial worlds.

H   nans use many methods for understanding our relationships with people, places, patterns, and processes. Our epistemologies include discursive and nondiscursive techniques. Key nondiscursive techniques include sensing, moving, embodying, and experiencing. Key discursive techniques that we use to understand and make biosocial worlds are storytelling and taxonomies. Understanding biosocial worlds involves putting conceptual boundaries around things, and then experimenting with where, when, and why those boundaries move. We forge our own stories and taxonomies out of the tools and materials at hand. Who we have to relate to, and how their behavior looks from our perspective, influence how we tell our stories and display our identities. Narratives about and classifications of ourselves and others change over time as our resources change, and our resources change because the stories we tell, or the ones we want to tell, influence how we interact with resources. The stories we tell about the relationships we have with people, places, patterns, and processes cause our epistemologies and our ecologies to be the fluid fields within which we forge our worlds, which means that our stories and taxonomies are also always under construction.

THE BIOSOCIAL SPACE-TIME MILIEU

Driven by his deep fascination with social networks, Christakis (2016) asks, "How do humans make networks with these ornate, reproducible patterns?" In his question, Christakis is saying that human social networks are the things that have ornate reproducible patterns. To apply Christakis's question to this study of the construction of biosocial milieu, we can twist the question around so that "ornate, reproducible patterns" refers to the sequential synchronies that humans recognize and then connect their own human activities to. In linking up with nonhuman entities' "ornate, reproducible patterns," humans construct not merely social networks composed of humans but also biosocial collectives consisting of multispecies and diverse entities. Christakis cites the numerous social network scholars who have found that humans "fare better and worse because we are connected to other [humans]" (Christakis 2016). We can extend his ideas to include nonhumans again so we can say that humans "fare better and worse because we are connected to" nonhumans. By coordinating our own customs with the routines of nonhumans, we "become" in sync with deeply interconnected networks. Social networks have memory, consistency, and resiliency which enable humans to experience more love and kindness, and to be happier and healthier (Christakis 2016). Taking off from Christakis's argument that "understanding the social network helps us understand health and emotions and lots of other things," we can say that understanding the biosocial milieu helps us to understand the phenomenological, interactional, and lots of other aspects of biosocial change. In the midst of constantly emerging novelties and continuously transitioning conditions, humans fare better when we have the flexibility to systematically shift subjectivities.

A pattern we find across cultures is that humans translate sequential synchronies into space-time cultures, yet the sequential synchronies that humans observe vary depending on their subjectivities which, in turn, lead to variations in the processes of interacting, consuming, classifying, experiencing, conceptualizing, embodying, communicating, and socializing. The lesson that humans perceive sequential synchronies in nature emerges from this book's exercise of shifting perspectives and looking for similarities and differences in the ways members of coherent social collectives perceive change. We observe differences in phenomenologies, interactions, and cosmologies across cultures, and we also see similarities. One cross-cultural pattern in space-time cultures is the recognition of sequential synchronies.

The meanings of "space-time" in geospatial science, astronomy, and anthropology converge in a biosocial theory about Kodi's biosocial worlds. That theory explains Kodi's biosocial worlds as consisting of diverse human and nonhuman actors, living organisms and nonliving entities, visible and invisible forces that mutually constitute one another as they engage in space-time involvements where they engineer one another's habitats and, over many generations, influence one another's evolution. Space-time is a frequently occurring concept in *Biosocial Synchrony on Sumba* because of its intriguing transdisciplinary relevance. Space-time is a standard term in geospatial analyses, astronomy, and it also appears in anthropology, though with much less frequency or standardization. In this particular ethnography, space-time refers to the dimensions where actors are involved with one another's activities and therefore affect the conditions of one another's existence. Because the actors who engage with one another impact abiotic and biotic ecologies and because they are involved in collectives that are at once ecological and social, their space-time involvements constitute biosocial milieu. Moreover, because humans have evolved as both biological and social beings, when all humans (Indigenous peoples, astronomers, marine biologists, anthropologists) interpret the space-time involvements they are privy to, they are constructing biosocial worlds.

In transhuman studies, scholars discuss the many ways humans seek to engineer biology (e.g., using reproductive technologies), or cognition (e.g., using artificial intelligence), or to enhance their experiences (e.g., using music) (Bostrom 2016). Human ideas and practices, according to transhumanists and biosocial theorists, can be intentional or unintentional and can enhance or degrade other entities. Biosocial theory differs from transhumanism in that it looks at how not only humans but also other types of entities change one another's beings and direct one another's evolution. Biosocial theory is more ecologically-holistic since its interests are in the mutual constitution of a much wider array of entities. Biosocial theory can take some cues from transhumanism, though, in developing explanations about human behaviors and beliefs relative to nonhumans. Where transhumanism talks about humans changing and enhancing human biologies, biosocial theorists can explain human beliefs and behaviors in terms of humans attempting to change and enhance many more types of beings: living humans, nonliving humans, human humans, nonhuman humans, and nonhumans. Thus, when Kodi chant and play drums for the multitude of Marapu ancestors and deities, they seek to intervene in naturecultures. In their *yaigho* healing rituals, for example, Kodi seek to intervene in disease ecologies. In their seaworm gathering rituals, Kodi seek to control fertility in animals, plants, and themselves. These are their ritual technologies for birthing, altering lives, handling emotions, avoiding hunger, and ensuring the survival of self and kin.

To claim your kinship to the Moon, Sun, pythons, crocodiles, rats, yams, *Bombax*, *Ceiba*, *Hibiscus*, and/or *Erythrina* is to possess a relational identity. To sense the lights in the sky or the sounds of cosmic gravity is to seek phenomenological interactions with extraterrestrial bodies. To schedule your own sleeping and waking upon the rising and setting of planets and stars is to pace your routines by the clock of astronomical entities. To consume seaworms is to become marine life. In engaging with the polychaetes, mimicking their swarming behaviors, consuming their bodies, and through other ways of relating to them, people become seaworms. Using the idea of "become" here references the theory of biosocial becomings (Ingold and Palsson 2013), and means that humans develop during their lifetimes in particular ways because of their relationships with nonhuman species. Polychaetes materially constitute the bodies of those humans who consume seaworms. The Moon and its chromatic rhythms partly determine the reproductive behaviors of polychaetes—which also influence the biological rhythms and courting behaviors of humans—and thus influence birth, death, and bodily modifications for spawning in polychaetes. To repeatedly and ritualistically recall the sacrifices your ancestors make to nourish you is to embody the fields where they are buried. To prioritize the expenditure of resources on fostering your relationships with all the souls who inhabit all of the world's subjects is to construct your own niche. The multispecies interactions that occur in Kodi have constructed the niches within which humans, polychaetes, local seascapes and landscapes, the vast universe, and all of the other entities who occupy past, present, and future space-time coevolve.

NOTES

1. This list of types of interactions is patterned upon Olff et al.'s (2009) list of six general types of interactions in ecological networks. Olff et al. (2009: n.p.) list the following: "(i) consumer-resource interactions, (ii) interactions between organisms and abiotic (non-resource) conditions, (iii) spatial interactions (inputs and outputs of energy, nutrients, organisms), (iv) non-trophic direct interactions among organisms, (v) physical and chemical interactions among factors/compartments, and (vi) external forcing of abiotic conditions." Olff et al.'s list contains some interactions that are not discussed in *Biosocial Synchrony on Sumba*, and it contains no social or cultural types of interactions. My list substitutes some relevant social and cultural types of interactions for those interactions that are not relevant in this book.

2. These lists of biotic and abiotic subjects in *Biosocial Synchrony on Sumba* is derived from Olff et al.'s (2009) list of six general types of biotic and abiotic compartments in ecological networks. Olff et al. (2009: n.p.) write: The "abiotic compartments are (i) abiotic resources (such as light, nitrate, ammonium, phosphate) that are consumed and depleted by autotrophs, (ii) abiotic conditions, that affect both autotrophs and heterotrophs but are not consumed or depleted by them (such as salinity, soil texture, sediment aeration, soil and water pH, temperature) but that can be modified (e.g., by ecosystem engineers [Jones, Lawton, and Shachak 1994; Lawton 1994]) and (iii) detritus (non-living organic material). The three main biotic compartments are (i) autotrophs that can harvest their own energy, either from light or chemical sources, (ii) microbial detrivores that break down detritus into its mineral components, thus producing resources for autotrophs and (iii) higher trophic levels that consume autotrophs, microbial detrivores and/or each other, and mineralize nutrients for autotrophs."

Works Cited

Aguado, M. Teresa, Guillermo San Martin, and Harry ten Hove. 2008. "Syllidae (Annelida: Polychaeta) from Indonesia Collected by the Siboga (1899–1900) and Snellius II (1984) Expeditions." *Zootaxa* 1673: 1–48.

Arditi, Roger, Jerzy Michalski, and Alexandre H. Hirzel. 2005. "Rheagogies: Mʌd-elling Non-trophic Effects in Food Webs." *Ecological Complexity* 2: 24ᵒ ⸝8. doi:10.1016/j.ecocom.2005.04.003.

Atkinson, Jane Monnig, and Shelly Errington, eds. 1990. *Power and Difference: Gender in Island Southeast Asia.* Palo Alto, CA: Stanford University Press.

Australian Museum. n.d. *Segemented Worms—The Polychaetes.* http://australian-museum.net.au/segmented-worms-the-polychaetes#How_do_polychaetes_reproduce_.

Barad, Karen. 2007. *Meeting the Universe Halfway: Quantum Physics and the Entanglement of Matter and Meaning.* Durham: Duke Unversity Press.

Bellwood, Peter. 2006. "Hierarchy, Founder Ideology, and Austronesian Expansion." In *Origins, Ancestry and Alliance: Explorations in Austronesian Ethnography,* edited by James J. Fox and Clifford Sather, 19–41. Canberra: Australian National University Press.

Bellwood, Peter, James J. Fox, and Darrell Tryon. 2006. *The Austronesians.* Canberra: Australian National University Press.

Bennett, Jane. 2010. *Vibrant Matter: A Political Ecology of Things.* Durham: Duke University Press.

Bentley, M. G., P. J. W. Olive, and Kay Last. 1999. "Sexual Satellites, Moonlight, and the Nuptial Dances of Worms: The Influence of the Moon on the Reproduction of Marine Animals." *Earth, Moon, and Planets* 85: 67–84.

Blust, Robert. 2008. "Is There a Bima-Sumba Subgroup?" *Oceanic Linguistics* 47(1): 45–113.

Blust, Robert, and Stephen Trussel. 2015. *The Austronesian Comparative Dictionary. Web Edition.* http://www.trussel2.com/acd/.

Bostrom, Nick. 2016. "Nick Bostrom's Home Page." http://www.nickbostrom.com/.

Burnaford, Jennifer L., Karina J. Nielsen, and Susan L. Williams. 2014. "Celestial Mechanics Affects Emersion Time and Cover Patterns of an Ecosystem Engineer, the Intertidal Kelp *Saccharina sessilis.*" *Marine Ecology Progress Series* 509: 127–136.

Caspers, H. 1984. "Spawning Periodicity and Habitat of the Palolo Worm Eunice viridis in the Samoan Islands." *Marine Biology* 79: 229–236.

Chaudhary, Zahid R. 2012. *Afterimage of Empire: Photography in Nineteenth-Century India.* Minneapolis: University of Minnesota Press.

Cheal, A. J., S. Delean, and S. Thompson. 2007. "Synchrony in Coral Reef Fish Populations and the Influence of Climate." *Ecology* 88(1): 158–169. doi: 10.1890/00129658 (2007)88[158:ssicrfj2.0.co;2.

Christakis, Nicholas. 2016. "How Do Our Social Networks Affects Our Health?" http://gpbnews.org/post/how-do-our-social-networks-affect-our-health.

Condominas, Georges. 1977. *We Have Eaten the Forest: The Story of a Montagnard Village in the Central Highlands of Vietnam.* Translated by Adrienne Foulke. New York: Hill and Wong.

Copeland, Jonathan, and Andrew Moiseff. 1994. "The Occurrence of Synchrony in the North American Firefly *Photinus carolinus* (Coleoptera: Lampyridae)." *Journal of Insect Behavior* 8(3): 381–394.

C ̇ks, J. A. 2002. "Characterizing Ecosystem-Level Consequences of Biological ̇sions: The Role of Ecosystem Engineers." *Oikos* 97: 153–166.

Daly, J. M. 1975. "Reversible Epitoky in the Life History of the Polychaete *Odontosyllis polycera* (Schmarda 1861)." *Journal of the Marine Biological Association of the United Kingdom* 55: 327.

Dammerman, K. W. 1926. "Flora en Fauna van Soemba." *De Tropische Natuur* May: 73–74.

Darwin, Charles. 1881. *The Formation of Vegetable Mould, through the Action of Worms, with Observations on their Habits.* London: Murray.

Descola, Philippe. 2014. "All Too Human (Still): A Comment on Eduardo Kohn's *How Forests Think.*" *HAU: Journal of Ethnographic Theory* 4(2): 267–273.

Durham, William H. 2002. "Cultural Variation in Time and Space: The Case for a Populational Theory of Culture." In *Anthropology Beyond Culture,* edited by Barbara J. King and Richard Gabriel Fox, 193–206. Oxford: Berg.

Earn, David J. D., Pejman Rohani, and Brian T. Grenfell. 1998. "Persistence, Chaos and Synchrony in Ecology and Epidemiology." *Proceedings of the Royal Society of London B* 265: 7–10.

Eicher, David J. 2016a. "The Screams of Black Holes." *Astronomy* 44(5): 6.

———. 2016b. "A Quasar Disappears." *Astronomy* 44(5): 17.

Eklund, Judith. "Marriage, Seaworms and Song: Ritualized Responses to Cultural Change in Sasak Life." PhD diss. Cornell University, 1977.

Endres, Klaus Peter, and Wolfgang Schad. 1997. *Moon Rhythms in Nature: How Lunar Cycles Affect Living Organisms.* Great Britain: Floris Books.

Fauvel, P. 1918. "Annélides Polychètes Nouvelles de l'Afrique Orientale." *Bulletin d'Muséum d'Histoire Naturelle, Paris* 24(7): 503–509.

Feral, P. 1989. "Biosedimentological Implications of the Polychaete *Lanice conchilega* (Pallas) on the Intertidal Zone of Two Norman Sandy Shores (France)." *Bulletin de la Société Géologique de France* 5: 1193–1200.

Fischer, A., and U. Fischer. 1995. "On the Life-Style and Life-Cycle of the Lumines-cent Polychaete *Odontosyllis enopla* (Annelida: Polychaeta)." *Invertebrate Biology* 114: 236.

Forth, Gregory. 1982. "Time and the Expression of Reality in Eastern Sumba." *Ethnos* 47: 232–248.

———. 1983. "Time and Temporal Classification in Rindi, Eastern Sumba." *Bijdragen tot de Taal-, Land- en Volkenkunde* 139(1): 46–80.

Fox, James J. 1979. "The Ceremonial System of Savu." In *The Imagination of Reality: Essays in Southeast Asian Coherence System*, edited by A. L. Becker and A. A. Yengoyan, 145–173. Norwood, NJ: Ablex.

———. 2006. "Postscript—Spatial Categories in Social Context: Taking a Comparative Understanding of Austronesian Ideas of Ritual Location." In *Sharing the Earth, Dividing the Land: Land and Territory in the Austronesian World*, edited by Thomas Reuter, 365–377. Canberra: ANU ePress.

Fowler, Cynthia. "The Creolization of Natives and Exotics: The Changing Symbolic and Functional Character of Culture and Agriculture in Kodi, West Sumba (Indonesia)." PhD diss. University of Hawai'i, 1999.

———. 2003. "The Ecological Implications of Ancestral Religion and Reciprocal Exchange in a Sacred Forest in Karendi." *World Views: Culture, Environment, Religion* 7(3): 303–329.

———. 2013. *Ignition Stories: Indigenous Fire Ecology in the Indo-Australian Monsoon Zone*. Durham: Carolina Academic Press.

———. 2015. "Wayfinding Women: The Generation of Landscapes through Female Entrepreneurship." *Urbanities* 5(1): 83–94.

Franknoi, Andrew. 2007. "How Fast Are You Moving When You Are Sitting Still?" *The Universe in the Classroom*, 71. https://astrosociety.org/edu/publications/tnl/71/howfast.html.

Gaston, Gary R., and Jennifer Hall. 2000. "Lunar Periodicity and Bioluminescence of Swarming *Odontosyllis luminosa* (Polychaeta: Syllidae) in Belize." *Gulf and Caribbean Research* 12: 47–51.

Geertz, Clifford. 1998. "Deep Hanging Out." *The New York Review of Books* October 22: 69–72.

Geinaert-Martin, Danielle C. 1992. *The Woven Land of Laboya Socio-Cosmic Ideas and Value sin West Sumba, Eastern Indonesia*. Leiden, The Netherlands: Centre of Non-Western Studies.

Glasby, Chris, and Kristian Fauchald. 2007. *POLiKEY*. Version 2. Last modified February 11, 2007. http://www.environment.gov.au/biodiversity/abrs/online-resources/polikey/.

Halanych, Kenneth N., L. Nicole Cox, and Torsten H. Struck. 2007. "A Brief Review of Holopelagic Annelids." *Integrative and Comparative Biology* 47(6): 872–879.

Hamer, K. C., J. K. Hill, L. A. Lace, and A. M. Langan. 1997. "Ecological and Biogeographical Effects of Forest Disturbance on Tropical Butterflies of Sumba, Indonesia." *Journal of Biogeography* 24: 67–75.

Harrison, P. L., R. C. Babcock, G. D. Bull, J. K. Oliver, C. C. Wallace, and B. L. Willis. 1984. "Mass Spawning in Tropical Coral Reefs." *Science* 223: 1186–1189.

Hartigan, John, Jr. 2015. *Aesop's Anthropology: A Multispecies Approach*. St. Paul, MN: University of Minnesota.

Hauenschild, C. 1960. "Lunar Periodicity." *Cold Spring Harbor Symposia on Quantitative Biology* 25: 491–497.

Haynes, Korey, and Eric Betz. 2016. "A Wrinkle in Space-Time Confirms Einstein's Gravitation." *Astronomy* May: 22–27. http://0-eds.a.ebscohost.com.library.wofford.edu/ehost/pdfviewer/pdfviewer?vid=2&sid=54546dde-ebbb-4e2e-84c5–36303db1 5acd%40sessionmgr4005&hid=4205.

Heaven's Above. 2016. *Planet Summary.* http://www.heavens-above.com/Planet-Summary.aspx?lat=-9.46&lng=119.09&loc=Sumba&alt=144&tz=UCTm8.

Herdobler, Bert, and Edward O. Wilson. 1990. *The Ants.* Cambridge, MA: Belknap Press.

Heyes, C. M. and B. G. Galaef. 1996. *Social Learning in Animals: The Roots of Culture.* San Diego: Academic Press.

Horst, R. 1902. "Over de 'Wawo' van Rumphius (*Lysidice oele*, n. sp.)." In *Rumphius Gedenkboek. 1702–1902.* Amsterdam: Koloniaal Museum Te Haarlem.

Hoskins, Janet Alison. 1985. "A Life History from Both Sides: The Changing Poetics of Personal Experience." *Journal of Anthropological Research* 41(2): 147–169.

———. 1988. "The Drum is My Shaman, the Spear Guides His Voice." *Social Science and Medicine* 27(8): 819–828.

———. 1990. Doubling Deities, Descent, and Personhood: An Exploration of Kodi Gender Categories. In Power and Difference: Gender in Island Southeast Asia. Jane Monnig Atkinson, and Shelly Errington, editors. Pages 273–306. Stanford University Press, Stanford.

———. 1993. *The Play of Time: Kodi Perspectives on Calendars, History, and Exchange.* Berkeley, CA: University of California Press.

———. 1996. "From Diagnosis to Performance: Medical Practice and the Politics of Exchange in Kodi, West Sumba." In *The Performance of Healing*, edited by Carol Laderman and Marina Roseman, 271–290. New York: Routledge.

———. 1998. *Biographical Objects: How Things Tell the Stories of People's Lives.* New York: Routledge.

Huntsman, A. G. 1948. "*Odontosyllis* at Bermuda and Lunar Periodicity." *Journal of the Fisheries Research Board of Canada* 7: 363.

Ingold, Tim. 2013. "Prospect." In *Biosocial Becomings: Integrating Social and Biological Anthropology*, edited by Tim Ingold and Gisli Palsson, 1–21. Cambridge: Cambridge University Press.

Ingold, Tim, and Gisli Palsson, eds. 2013. *Biosocial Becomings: Integrating Social and Biological Anthropology.* Cambridge: Cambridge University Press.

Jensen, Ole B. 2010. "Erving Goffman and Everyday Life Mobility." In *The Contemporary Goffman*, edited by Michale H. Jacobsen, 333–351. New York: Routledge.

Jones, Clive G., J. H. Lawton, M. Shachak. 1994. "Organisms as Ecosystem Engineers." *Oikos* 69: 373–386.

Keck, Frédéric. 2013. "Eduardo Kohn's How Forests Think: Toward an Anthropology Beyond the Human." *Somatosphere: Science, Medicina and Anthropology* (blog), September 23, 2013. http://somatosphere.net/2013/09/eduardo-kohns-how-forests-think.html.

Kennedy, B., and J. S. Pearse. 1975. "Lunar Synchronization of the Monthly Reproductive Rhythm in the Sea Urchin *Centrostephanus coronatus* Verrill." *Journal of Experimental Marine Biology and Ecology* 17: 323–331.

Kirch, Patrick Vinton, and Roger Green. 2001. *Hawaiki, Ancestral Polynesia: An Essay in Historical Anthropology*. Cambridge: Cambridge University Press.

Kirksey, Eben. n.d. *Swarm*. http://www.multispecies-salon.org/swarm/.

Kirksey, Eben, Craig Schuetze, and Stefan Helmreich. 2014. "Introduction." In *Multispecies Salon*, edited by Eben Kirksey, 1–24. Durham: Duke University Press.

Knight, John. 2005. *Animals in Person: Cultural Perspectives on Human-Animal Intimacy*. London: Bloomsbury Academic.

Koenig, Walter D., Johannes M. H. Knops, William J. Carmen, and Mark T. Stanback. 1999. "Spatial Dynamics in the Absence of Dispersal: Acorn Production by Oaks in Central Coastal California." *Ecography* 22: 499–506.

Kohn, Eduardo. 2007. "How Dogs Dream: Amazonian Natures and the Politics of Transspecies Engagements." *American Ethnologist* 34(1): 2–34.

———. 2013. *How Forests Think: Toward an Anthropology Beyond the Human*. Berkeley: University of California Press.

Kosek, Jake. 2010. "Ecology of Empire: On the New Uses of Honeybees." *Cultural Anthropology* 25(4): 650–678.

Kubota, Tomoyuki. 2005. "Reproduction in the Apodid Sea Cucumber *Patinapta ooplax*: Semilunar Spawning Cycle and Sex Change." *Zoological Science* 17(1): 75–81.

Laland, Kevin. 2013. "Human Cultural Niche Construction and the Social Sciences." In *Encyclopedia of Philosophy and the Social Sciences*, edited by Byron Kaldis, 433–435. Thousand Oaks, CA: Sage Publications.

Lansing, J. Stephen, Murray P. Cox, Sean S. Downey, Brandon M. Gabler, Brian Hallmark, Tatiana M. Karafet, Peter Norquest, John W. Schoenfelder, Herawati Sudoyo, Joseph C. Watkins, and Michael F. Hammer. 2007. "Coevolution of Languages and Genes on the Island of Sumba, Eastern Indonesia." *Proceedings of the National Academy of Science* 104(41): 16022–16026.

Lattig, Patricia, Daniel Martin, and M. Teresa Aguado. 2010. "Four New Species of *Haplosyllis* (Polychaeta: Syllidae: Syllinae) from Indonesia." *Journal of the Marine Biological Association of the United Kingdom* 90(4): 789–798.

Leibhold, Andrew, Naoto Kamata, and Thomas Jacob. 1996. "Cyclicity and Synchrony of Historical Outbreaks of Beech Caterpillar *Quadricalcarifera punctatella* (Mostchulsky) in Japan." *Researches on Population Ecology* 38(1): 87–94.

Leibhold, Andrew, Walter D. Koenig, and Ottar N. Bjørnstad. 2004. "Spatial Synchrony in Population Dynamics." *Annual Review of Ecology and Evolutionary Systematics* 35: 467–490.

Lewis, Sara M., Lynn Faust, and Raphael De Cock. 2012. "The Dark Side of the Light Show: Predators of Fireflies in the Great Smoky Mountains." *Psyche: Journal of Entomology* 2012: 1–7.

Lindström, Jan, Essa Ranta, and Harto Lindén. 1996. "Large-Scale Synchrony in the Dynamics of Capercallie, Black Grouse, and Hazel Grouse Populations in Finland." *Oikos* 76(2): 221–227.

Loreau, Michel, and Claire de Mazancourt. 2008. "Species Synchrony and Its Drivers: Neutral and Nonneutral Community Dynamics in Fluctuating Environments." *The American Naturalist* 172(2): E48–E66. doi: 10.11086/589746.

Mackin-Rogalska, R., and L. Nabaglo. 1990. "Geographical Variation in Cyclic Periodicity and Synchrony in the Common Vole, *Microtus arvalis*." *Oikos* 59: 343–348.

McWilliam, Andrew. 2006. "Fataluku Forest Tenures and the Conis Santana National Park in East Timor." In *Sharing the Earth, Dividing the Land: Land and Territory in the Austronesian World*, edited by Thomas Reuter, 253–275. Canberra: ANU ePress.

Meadows, P. S., A. Meadows, and J. M. H. Murray. 2012. "Biological Modifiers of Marine Benthic Seascapes: Their Role as Ecosystem Engineers." *Geomorphology* 157: 31–48.

Menge, Bruce A., Francis Chan, Sarah Dudas, Dafne Eerkes-Medrano, Kirsten Grorud-Colvert, Kimberly Heiman, Margot Hessing-Lewis, Alison Iles, Ruth Milston-Clements, Mae Noble, Kimberly Page-Albins, Erin Richmond, Gil Rilov, Jeremy Rose, Joe Tyburczy, Luis Vinueza, and Phoebe Zarnetske. 2009. "Terrestrial Ecologists Ignore Aquatic Literature: Assymetry in Citation Breadth in Ecological Publications and Implications for Generality and Progress in Ecology." *Journal of Experimental Marine Biology and Ecology* 377(2): 93–100.

Mercier, Annie, and Jean-Francios Hamel. 2015. "Lunar Periods in the Annual Reproductive Cycles of Marine Invertebrates from Cold Subtidal and Deep-Sea Environments." In *Annual, Lunar, and Tidal Clocks: Patterns and Mechanisms of Nature's Enigmatic Rhythms*, edited by Hideharu Numata and Barbara Helm, 99–120. Tokyo: Springer.

Meyer, William B., and B. L. Turner II. 1994. *Changes in Land Cover and Land Use: A Global Perspective*. Cambridge: Cambridge University Press.

Mondragon, Carlos. 2004. "Of Winds, Worms and *Mana*: The Traditional Calendar of the Torres Islands, Vanuatu." *Oceania* 74(4): 289–308.

Moran, P. A. P. 1953. "The Statistical Analysis of the Canandian Lynx Cycle II: Synchronization and Meteorology." *The Australian Journal of Zoology* 1: 291–298. doi: 10.1071/zo9530291.

Munn, Nancy. 1973. *Walbiri Iconography: Graphic Representation and Cultural Symbolism in a Central Australian Society*. Chicago: University of Chicago Press.

Murphy, Megan A., Nathan L. Thompson, and Johanes Shul. 2016. "Keeping up with the Neighbor: A Novel Mechanism of Call Synchrony in Neoconocephalus ensiger Katydids." *Journal of Comparative Physiology* 202(3): 225–234.

Myers, Judith H. 1990. "Population Cycles of Western Tent Caterpillars: Experimental Introductions and Synchrony of Fluctuations." *Ecology* 71(3): 986–985.

Norquest, Peter, and Sean Downey. 2013. "Expanding the PAN Consonant Inventory." *Journal of Southeast Asian Linguistics Society* 6: 99–145.

O'Meara, Stephen James. 2016. "Listen to the Stars." *Astronomy* May: 20. http://www.astronomy.com/magazine/stephen-omeara/2016/03/listen-to-the-stars.

Odling-Smee, F. John, Kevin N. Laland, and Marcus W. Feldman. 2013. "Niche Construction: The Neglected Process in Evolution." *Monographs in Population Biology*, Volume 37. Princeton: Princeton University Press.

Olff, Han, David Alonso, Matty P. Berg, B. Klemmons Eriksson, Michel Loreau, Theunis Piersma, and Neil Rooney. 2009. "Parallel Ecological Networks in Ecosystems." *Philosophical Transactions B* 364(1524): 1755–1779.

Orr, Yancey, J. Stephen Lansing, and Michael R. Dove. 2015. "Environmental Anthropology: Systemic Perspectives." *Annual Review of Anthropology* 44: 153–168.

Orr, Yancey. 2016. "Semiotics and the Specter of Taboo: The Perception and Interpretation of Dogs and Rabies in Bali, Indonesia." *American Anthropologist* 118(1): 67–77. doi: 10.1111/aman.12448.

Palmer, Lisa, and Demetrio do Amaral de Carvalho. 2008. "Nature Building and Resource Management: The Politics of 'Nature' in Timor Leste." *Geoforum* 39: 1321–1332.

Palsson, Gisli. 2013. "Ensembles of Biosocial Relations." In *Biosocial Becomings: Integrating Social and Biological Anthropology*, edited by Tim Ingold and Gisli Palsson, 22–41. Cambridge: Cambridge University Press.

Pamungkas, Joko, and Christopher J. Glasby. 2015. "Taxonomy of Reproductive Nereididae (Annelida) in Multispecies Swarms at Ambon Island, Indonesia." *Zookeys* 520: 1–25.

Pitrou, Perig. 2015. "An Anthropology Beyond Nature and Culture? Tim Ingold and Gisli Palsson's Edited Volume, Biosocial Becomings." *Somatosphere: Science, Medicina and Anthropology* (blog), August 5, 2015. Translated by Daniela Ginsburg. http://somatosphere.net/2015/08/an-anthropology-beyond-nature-and-culture-tim-ingold-and-gisli-palssons-edited-volume-biosocial-becomings.html.

Plotkin, Pamela T., David C. Rostal, Richard A. Byles, and David W. Owens. 1997. "Reproductive and Development Synchrony in Female *Lepidochelys olivacea*." *Journal of Herpetology* 31(1): 17–22.

Rabaut, M., M. Vincx, and S. Degraer. 2009. "Do *Lanice conchilega* (Sandma n) Aggregations Classify as Reefs? Quantifying Habitat Modifying Effects." *go-land Marine Research* 63: 37–46.

Radjawane, T. R. 1982. *Laor: Cacing Laut Khas Perairan Maluku*. Jakarta: Lomba Karya Penelitian Ilmiah Remajah, Jakarta, Departemen Pendidikan dan Kebudayaan Republik Indonesia.

Read, Geoffrey, and Kristian Fauchald, eds. 2015. *World Polychaeta Database*. Page generated on August 12, 2016. http://www.marinespecies.org/polychaeta.

Rosenstock, Todd S., Alan Hastings, Walter D. Koenig, Danielle J. Lyles, and Patrick H. Brown. 2011. "Testing Moran's Theorem in Agroecosystems." *Oikos* 120(9): 1434–1440.

Russell, Frederick S., and Maurice Yonge. 1974. *Advances in Marine Biology*. London: Academic Press, Inc.

Salazar-Vallejo, Sergio I., Luis F. Carrera-Parra, Alexander I. Muir, Jesus Angel de Leon Gonzalez, Christina Piotrowski, and Masanori Sato. 2014. "Polychaete Species (Annelid) Described from The Philippine and China Seas." *Zootaxa Monograph* 3842: 001–068. Auckland, New Zealand: Magnolia Press.

Samoilys, M., and G. Carlos. 1990. *A Survey of Reef Fish Stocks in Western Samoa: Application of Underwater Visual Census Methods. A Report Prepared for the Forum Fisheries Agency, Honiara, Solomon Islands and the Government of Samoa*. Field Report No. 6. FAO/UNDP SAM/89/002.

Schulze, Anja. 2006. "Phylogeny and Genetic Diversity of Palolo Worms (Palola, Eunicidae) from the Tropical North Pacific and the Caribbean." *Biological Bulletin* 210(1): 25–37.

Schulze, Anja, and Laura Timm. 2012. "*Palolo* and *Un*: Distinct Clades in the Genus *Palola* (Eunicidae, Polychaeta)." *Marine Biodiversity* 42(2): 161–171.

Scott, Emily, and James B. Wood, eds. n.d. *Marine Invertebrates of Bermuda*. http://www.thecephalopodpage.org/MarineInvertebrateZoology/Odontosyllisenopla1.html.

Scov, Martin W., Richard G. Hartnoll, Renison K. Ruwa, Jude P. Shunula, Marco Vannini, and Stefano Cannicci. 2005. "Marching to a Different Drummer: Crabs Synchronize Reproduction to a 14-Month Lunar-Tidal Cycle." *Ecology* 86(5): 1164–1171.

Singer, Francis J., Wayne T. Swank, and Edward E. C. Clebsch. 1984. "Effects of Wild Pig Rooting in a Deciduous Forest." *Journal of Wildlife Management* 48(2): 464–473.

Smith, David Woodruff. 2013. "Phenomenology." In *The Stanford Encyclopedia of Philosophy*, edited by Edward N. Zalta. Last modified December 13, 2013. http://plato.stanford.edu/archives/win2013/entries/phenomenology/.

Springer, Simon. n.d. *Earth Writing*. https://www.academia.edu/4876496/Earth_ Writing.

Stair, John B. 1897. "Palolo: A Sea-Worm Eaten by the Samoans." *Journal of the Polynesian Society* 6: 141–144.

Stewart, Pamela J., and Andrew Strathern. 2000. *The Python's Back: Pathways of Comparison Between Indonesia and Melanesia*. Santa Cruz: Praeger Publishers.

Sweeney, Alison M., Charles A. Boch, Sonke Johnson, and Daniel E. Morse. 2011. "Twilight Spectral Dynamics and the Coral Reef Invertebrate Spawning `esponse." *Journal of Experimental Biology* 214: 770–777.

T. ibaum, Nicola, and Carnelia Ann Kammerer, eds. 2006. *Founders' Cults in Sc...heast Asia: Ancestors, Polity, and Identity*. New Haven, CT: Yale Southeast Asia Studies.

Tarnas, Richard. 2006. *Cosmos and Psyche*. New York: Penguin Group.

ten Hove, H. A., and A. K. Kupriyanova. 2009. "Taxonomy of Serpulidae (Annelida, Polychaeta): The State of Affairs." *Zootaxa* 36: 1–126.

Thacker, Eugene. 2004. *Networks, Swarms, Multitudes*. http://www.ctheory.net/articles.aspx?id=422.

Thompson, John N. 2005. *The Geographic Mosaic of Coevolution*. Chicago: University of Chicago Press.

Tsing, Anna. 2015. *In the Midst of Disturbance: Symbiosis, Coordination, History, Landscape*. http://www.theasa.org/downloads/publications/firth/firth15.pdf.

Tyson, Neil deGrasse, Charles Liu, and Robert Irion. 2000. *One Universe: At Home in the Cosmos*. Washington: National Academies Press. doi: 10.17226/9585.

Ulanowicz, R. E. 1997. *Ecology, the Ascendent Perspective*. New York: Columbia University Press.

Van Wey, Leah K., Elinor Ostrom, and Vicky Meretsky. 2005. "Theories Underlying the Study of Human-Environment Interactions." In *Seeing the Forest and the Trees: Human-Environment Interactions in Forest Ecosystems*, edited by Emilio F. Moran and Elinor Ostrom, 23–56. Cambridge, MA: MIT Press.

Verheijen, J. A. J. 1984. "Plant Names in Austronesian Linguistics." *Nusa: Linguistic Studies of Indonesian and Other Languages in Indonesia* 20: 0–98.

Victor, B. C., G. M. Wellington, D. R. Robertson, and B. I. Ruttenberg. 2001. "The Effect of the El Niño-Southern Oscillation Event on the Distribution of

Reef-Associated Labrid Fishes in the Eastern Pacific Ocean." *Bulletin of Marine Science* 69(1): 279–288.

Vitousek, Peter M., Lawrence R. Walker, Lewis D. Whiteaker, Deiter Mueller-Dumbois, and Pamela A. Matson. 1987. "Biological Invasion by *Myrica faya* Alters Ecosystem Development in Hawaii." *Science* 238: 802–804.

Viveiros de Castro, Eduardo. 2014. *Cannibal Metaphysics.* Translated by Peter Skafish. Minneapolis: Univocal Publishing.

Wassman, Jürg, and Pierre R. Dasen. 2000. "Balinese Spatial Orientation: Some Empirical Evidence of Modest Linguistic Relativity." *Journal of the Royal Anthropological Institute* 4: 689–711.

Welker, Marina A. 2009. "'Corporate Security Begins in the Community': Mining, the Corporate Social Responsibility Industry, and Environmental Advocacy in Indonesia." *Cultural Anthropology* 24(1): 142–179.

Whitehead, Neil L. 2009. "Posthuman Anthropology." *Identities: Global Studies in Culture and Power* 16(1): 1–32.

Wilkens, Lon A., and Jerome J. Wolken. 1981. "Electroretinograms from *Odontosyllis enopla* (Polychaeta: Syllidae): Initial Observations on the Visual System of the Bioluminescent Fireworm of Bermuda." *Marine Behavior and Physiology* 8(1): 55–66.

Williams, Kathy S., Kimberly G. Smith, and Frederick M. Stephen. 1993. "Emergence of 13-Year Periodical Cicadas (Cicadidae: Magicicada): Phenology, Mortality, and Predator Satiation." *Ecology* 74(4): 1143–1152.

Williams, Robert. 1996. "Hubble's Deepest View of the Universe Unveils Bewildering Galaxies Across Billions of Years." *Hubblesite.* http://hubblesite.org/newscenter/archive/releases/1996/01/image/a/.

Wilmer, Pat. 2012. "Ecology: Pollinator-Plant Synchrony Tested by Climate Change." *Current Biology* 22(4): R131–R132. doi: 10.1016/j.cub.2012.01.009.

World Conservation Monitoring Centre. 1996. "Eunice viridis." *The IUCN Red List of Threatened Species.* http://dx.doi.org/10.2305/IUCN.UK.1996.RLTS.T8261A12903350.en.

Wright, Justin P., and Clive G. Jones. 2006. "The Concept of Organisms as Ecosystem Engineers Ten Years On: Progress, Limitations, and Challenges." *BioScience* 56(3): 203–209.

Wu, Yan-Yi. "The Mechanism of Semilunar Swarming Rhythm in *Perinereis aibuhitensis* (Polychaeta)." Master's thesis, National Sun Yat-sen University, 2014.

Yan, Chuan, Neils Stenseth, Charles J. Krebs, and Zhibin Zhang. 2013. "Linking Climate Change to Population Cycles of Hares and Lynx." *Global Change Biology* 19(11): 3263–3271. doi: 10.1111/gcb.12321.

Yates-Doerr, Emily. 2015. "Does Meat Come from Animals? A Multispecies Approach to Classification and Belonging in Highland Guatemala." *American Ethnologist* 42(2): 309–323.

Zulkifly, Shahrizim B., James M. Graham, Erica B. Young, Robert J. Mayer, Michael J. Piotrowski, Izak Smith, and Linda E. Graham. 2013. "The Genus *Cladophora* Kützing (Ulvophyceae) as Globally Distributed Ecological Engineer." *Journal of Phycology* 49: 1–17.

Index

Note: Page references for figures are italicized.

About the Author

Dr. Cynthia "Cissy" Fowler is on the faculty of the Department of Sociology and Anthropology at Wofford College in South Carolina where she teaches courses in the subdisciplines of cultural, ecological, and medical anthropology, as well as courses on ethnography, ethnographic film, cultures of Southeast Asia and Oceania, global health, and diversity. Dr. Fowler serves as the Society of Ethnobiology's President Elect and is a founder and editorial board member for the open source journal *Ethnobiology ʾt-ters*. Fowler's research interests are in the areas of space-time culture and biosocial dynamics. She has conducted ethnographic fieldwork in Indonesia, Hawai'i, and the U.S. South. Fowler has published her research results in journal articles and books. Dr. Fowler is the coeditor of the monograph series Global Change/Global Health published by the University of Arizona Press. Fowler received her PhD from the University of Hawai'i, and her MA and BA from the University of Georgia.